And Then...God Showed Me His Love

And Then...God Showed Me His Love

TRACEY A. SCOTT

ISBN: 1512111864
ISBN 13: 9781512111866
Library of Congress Control Number: 2015907804
CreateSpace Independent Publishing Platform
North Charleston, South Carolina

This book is lovingly dedicated to

Jesus,

my Lord and Savior, who called me to write this book. He is my everything.

My Family,

my husband, Sean; my daughters, Brittini and Alysha; my son, Seanny;
and my sons-in-law, Ray and Christopher.
Their love and support have made this book possible.
They are the jewels in my crown.

My Partners,

my family, my mom, my mother- and father-in-law,
Aunt Diane, Marla, and all who supported me financially and through prayers.
There are just too many to name.

Introduction

This book is a calling that God placed on my heart years ago. I didn't know how to start it or even what to write. After many failed attempts, I had pretty much given up. But God isn't in favor of letting dreams die. Through countless people encouraging me to write my story, I knew it was God's will. Still, every time I sat down to write…nothing would come.

God very gently told me that my pride was in the way. I wasn't sure what He was talking about since I have never thought very highly of myself. He told me I was not willing to share my entire story, failures and all. Fear and pride kept corners of my life hidden. He said if I were willing to let my life be an open book, He would use it to bring redemption, restoration, and healing to many. My book would break bondages in people's lives.

I humbly repented and told God that if He could use my testimony for His glory and could use my story to bring healing, I would tell it. All of it.

I understood what God was talking about in 2 Corinthians 12:9. "My Grace is sufficient for you, for My power is made perfect in weakness." When I didn't have the power or ability to do something, that's when God's power shined through. I can't take the credit for anything…it's all Him.

You see, when God showed me His love, what people thought of me didn't matter anymore. In the Bible, Jesus says, "Those who have been forgiven little love little. But those who have been forgiven much love much."

I have been forgiven much, and I love *much*. I don't want anyone carrying burdens, guilt, and shame. I don't want anyone to feel hopeless. As you read, ask God to reveal His truth to you. Most of all, let His unconditional love overwhelm you as it did me.

So I humbly present to you my story…

Chapter 1

On July 7, 1990, I married the man of my dreams—really, I did. Only ten short months before this, I wrote God a list of qualities I wanted in a husband, and Sean fulfilled them all. I wanted a man who was Christian, strong, good-looking, protective, and athletic. Of course, what does a nineteen-year-old really know about what she needs in a lifetime commitment? At the time, I thought everything.

I met Sean in November of 1989. I was going through a pretty hard time in my life. I didn't think there was much good about me. From the time I was young, I had men ruin my trust, innocence, and self-esteem. Not that I ever had much self-esteem anyway, but what little I had was taken and crushed. I always knew I wasn't the pretty one in my family. I was definitely not the smartest and not the most athletic, but I was told I had a good personality—just what every girl wants to hear. Then multiple men made it clear to me that I was only good for one thing. They showed me what I was worth. I had deep wounds that were not visible to the human eye. With being abused, hit, and rejected, I had started to believe the lie. Did you ever notice how easy it is to believe lies over the truth?

I hated giving speeches in high school and college. Having to get up in front of a group of people and speak was just plain awful. I had always talked softly and quickly, but when eyes were upon me, it intensified. I knew that no one heard what I was saying. They were just looking at me and seeing all my imperfections. I always got Bs and Cs on those speeches. My teachers and professors said the written reports were good, but they had no idea what I was saying. That was fine with me. I knew I could get As on the tests to make up for it.

I dated a lot. I loved the attention guys gave me on the first couple of dates. I felt so special. Plus, money was always tight, so at least I got a free meal out of it. But after a date or two, they usually made me feel like I owed them and would try to force themselves on me. So I would move on to someone else. I kept thinking that I would eventually find a guy who could see my heart and appreciate me. I thought a guy would complete me. Somehow I would always pick the "winners." I did date a few nice guys, but I didn't know how to receive their love. It was easier for me to accept the abuse and rejection. I remember the first time a guy hit me. I was so shocked and mad; I stormed back to my dorm room. Tears burned my eyes. How dare someone treat me that way. But then a little voice inside of me from my long-ago past said, "You know you deserved it." So many memories came crashing down on me. I was instantly thrown back to a time when I was in high school and an older Christian man took advantage of me. I knew I was somehow to blame; I mean he was loved and respected by everyone. Who was I? The lie started to grow roots. So I continued to see the guy who hit me, and the abuse continued. I finally had enough when I caught him in bed with another girl. He had threatened me in multiple ways if I ever left him. If he wanted to kill me for leaving him, I didn't care anymore. Surprisingly, he moved on rather quickly, which didn't exactly do wonders for my ego.

I would like to say these were the worst things that happened to me, but they weren't. It's funny how you can shut off your feelings and emotions. I guess it was my body's way of coping. I never really talked to people about what was going on in my life or things that had happened in my childhood. I was taught to be stoic and keep my feelings and private life to myself. I had so many buried secrets and hurts. I guess to other people, I looked like everything was fine. People thought of me as a "good girl." I felt like dirt. I was two different people: the one other people saw and the person I was inside.

After more abuse and guys repeatedly telling me I was only good for one thing, I decided to write God a list of qualities I wanted in my future husband. A month later, I met Sean Scott. He was such a gentleman and was so good-looking. The first thing I noticed about him was how ripped his forearms were. I was working in the mall at a store that sold pianos when Sean first noticed me. Over the next couple of weeks, he seemed to be at the mall a lot. One evening, a couple of hours before closing time, Sean finally asked me out. I actually had a date with someone else that night, but I decided to stand him up. When Sean came to pick me up for our first date, he insisted on carrying my purse and coat for me. I was embarrassed for him. I mean here was a young and rugged man carrying a woman's purse and coat through a mall. It didn't bother him in the least. As he was opening the door for me, I thought, *Here is a guy who is secure in who he is and is a real gentleman.* We went out to dinner, and the first thing he asked me was if I was a Christian. I really hit the jackpot! His first concern was if I loved the Lord.

We went back to my home, and when I introduced him to my family, my dad realized that he had coached Sean in little league baseball. We had even given him rides back home after games. I didn't remember any of this, but I thought, *Okay, he must be somewhat athletic, too.* He was meeting all the requirements on my list. I was falling in love with him on our first date!

We watched a movie alone and talked for hours. Neither of us wanted the night to end. As I walked him to the door, he asked if he could kiss me good night. Of course I said yes. Then he told me he'd see me the next day and was gone. He didn't pressure me, didn't force himself on me, and didn't make me feel like I owed him anything. I barely slept that night. I had to be up early the next morning for work and then was heading back to college. Sean unexpectedly came to pick me up at work and take me back to school. We were inseparable from that point on. He was so courteous and protective of me. After a couple of weeks, he told me he was falling in love with me. Good, because I had already fallen in love with him. I always had a hard time expressing myself through words, but Sean seemed to understand me and how I felt.

It was now December 1989. I love Christmas. If I had my way, I'd put my Christmas decorations up in October. Being in college, I didn't have extra money for much, especially Christmas decorations. One day I came back to my dorm room between classes, and there was a Christmas tree fully decorated and lit up! It was beautiful. Sean had snuck in and put up a tree. I was so proud that he was my boyfriend. I was starting to get worried, though. If I wanted any kind of future with Sean, I had to tell him some of my past. I knew that once I told him some of the awful things about me, our relationship would end. So shortly after Christmas, I had a talk with him. He was so patient and understanding. He told me my past wasn't my fault. He told me he loved me for who I am today. I could not believe what I was hearing. He saw the beauty in me when I didn't think there was any to see. A week later, he proposed to me. I was floating; my prince had come to take me away.

Everyone thought we were rushing things, but we were in love. Sean never gave me ultimatums or pressured me. I wanted to show him how much I loved him, and I knew what I was good for. Men had made sure I'd known that since I was young. We had such a romantic night, and I didn't feel bad or guilty. We were getting married, after all. We set a wedding date for July 7, 1990. Life was good.

It was a couple of weeks before Valentine's Day, and I wasn't feeling well. I was so tired and sick. I could feel a wave of fear sweep over me, the kind you can't shake or reason away. My period was late. I felt like I couldn't breathe. *Oh, dear God, please don't let me be pregnant.* I walked to the nearest drug store and bought a pregnancy test. I got back to my dorm and went straight to the bathroom to take the test. *I'm not pregnant…I'm not pregnant…I'm not pregnant.* I figured if I thought it enough, I wouldn't be. With shaking hands, I picked up the test and froze. It was positive. In one second, my life changed forever. I remembered my mom telling me if I ever got pregnant out of wedlock, I would break my dad's heart. The room was spinning. I had just ruined so many lives.

What was Sean going to think? How was he going to react? I went back to my room and cried. When Sean came to visit me that evening, I gave him the news. I could tell he was shocked and hurt. I cried some more, which I rarely did in front of people. He said I could have an abortion. What? He could not be serious. Then he explained the options. He said we weren't financially ready to have a child. It would suffer because of us. We would hurt and shame our parents. If we had an abortion, no one would even know. And if I had one soon, it wasn't really a baby yet. He made so much sense to me. I agreed it was the best option. He helped me make an appointment for a week later to have our "situation" taken care of. He unfortunately couldn't get the day off of work, so I went without him. Down deep, this caused bitterness in me toward Sean. He could distance himself, but I couldn't. I would be the one with all the haunting memories.

There were so many women at the clinic. There was an eerie silence in the waiting room. No one said anything to me as they escorted me back to an exam room, and within a short period of time, I was out in the recovery room. I was so scared and numb. I sat there just staring at everyone else. I was having trouble blinking. Some of the women were laughing and talking. I couldn't even open my mouth. What had I done? I just made the biggest mistake of my life.

"Please, God, take me half an hour back in time and let me change my actions. Please, God, I am so sorry," I begged Him.

Now not only was I worthless, but I was a murderer. For once, the little voice inside of me wasn't condemning me. It now whispered to me, "It's over; forget about it and move on."

I didn't realize that was impossible. There was a deep, gaping wound that only my Creator could fix. I don't remember much about that day after that. When I saw Sean later that evening, he asked me how I was. I couldn't tell him how I was feeling. I didn't want to disappoint him, and, besides, I was taught to keep my feelings to myself. I could tell he didn't want to talk about it anymore than I did. So I didn't give him the chance to help me heal, if that was even possible. My heart was broken, probably forever.

We continued to plan our wedding. We were still so in love. I buried my guilt and hurt and focused on the future. Deep down, my heart ached. Not talking about it made the wound even bigger. I was so ashamed and broken. Even though life was wonderful in so many ways, there was a part of me that couldn't be happy. I didn't deserve to be. Did you ever notice that self-inflicted pain hurts worse than when someone else hurts you? I was a selfish, disgusting person. I kept silent, though. If I kept quiet about it, then it didn't happen in the rest of the world's eyes. So I suffered in silence. I created my own prison.

On our wedding day, I wore a beautiful white gown. Really?! Why did I do that? When I saw Sean at the front of the church waiting for me, I felt a glimmer of happiness again. I was marrying the man I loved and who loved mc for me. Sean was a man who knew most of my deep, dark secrets and said "I do" anyway. We didn't stay at the reception long. Sean swept me up and carried me to the car. We didn't have much money, so we stayed at a place about an hour away for a few days. We had a fun and relaxing time, and I started to feel like life was good again.

What I didn't realize was how much baggage we each brought into our marriage. We both were broken in so many ways. We figured if we didn't talk about the past, it would just disappear and wouldn't affect us now. Sean had so much anger, and I had so much bitterness and so many insecurities. So we built our marriage on sand. Whenever we had a problem, instead of dealing with just that issue, we would bring up nasty details about our pasts. Sean would say such mean and hurtful things, and I would just withdraw and become cold and distant. We didn't understand it then, but we were just digging our pit deeper and deeper. We always made up and apologized, though. We really did love each other; we just didn't know how to heal.

We talked about having children. Sean wanted to wait five years; I only wanted to wait two years. We were only nineteen and twenty, so there was no hurry. Well, after being married for three months, I found out I was pregnant. We were scared and excited at the same time. God, in His great mercy, granted me another child. I thought constantly about my first baby. I felt bad about being excited for this baby. *How come I want a baby now when only eight short months ago I didn't?* But I was excited nonetheless. From my ultrasound, I found out I was having a baby girl. I wanted her middle name to be Arlene. My grandma, mom, and I all have that middle name, so I wanted to pass it on. I told Sean he could pick her first name. He decided on the name Ashley.

It was a rough pregnancy, with a few scares and complications, but on May 31, 1991, our baby girl was born. When Sean looked at her, he said, "Her name is Brittini Arlene." I still don't know what made him change the name he had picked out, but Brittini was beautiful in every way. I was extremely sick the first few weeks after I had her. I was so young and thin; I was five-foot seven and weighed ninety-five pounds. I was always too skinny, but now I was having trouble eating. I was dehydrated and had some infections going on. I finally started to feel better, and I became unbelievably protective of Brittini. She was my precious gift, and no one could take care of her like I could.

Sean and I became even more distant. He no longer had much patience for me, and I didn't have much time for him. When Brittini was a couple of months old, we separated. Could I be a bigger failure? I wanted the perfect marriage but had no idea how to make it happen. I was hurt, but my heart had slowly been turning to stone over the years, so it wasn't a deep wound. Whatever. If he didn't want me anymore, that was just fine. Brittini and I could face the world together. But the very next day, Sean called me and profusely apologized. We talked a lot for a week. I still loved him, so we got back together. What we didn't realize is that we hadn't fixed anything. We slapped a Band-Aid over the hurts and wounds and moved on.

One day when Brittini was three months old, I woke up in a lot of pain. We went to the doctor's office, and I found out I had a miscarriage. I felt bad, but I didn't feel the overwhelming heartache like I did when I had an abortion. At least it wasn't my fault. I hoped I hadn't done anything to cause it. Still, my heart yearned to know details about the children I had lost. How I wish I could have held them at least once.

That November of 1991, Sean went into the police academy. He was gone for five months, and I only got to see him a few times. It was a difficult period, but we were excited to start fresh. We had been so poor up until this point, and what little we had went straight to Brittini. I went without meals, usually eating once a day, to help make ends meet. I knew Sean had it rough at the academy, but I knew they were at least feeding him. I got to go to his graduation in March 1992. He was even asked to give a speech. I was so proud of him, and we were so in love. I just knew from this point on life was going to be easy and good.

Well, I found out a couple of months later that I had gotten pregnant the night of Sean's graduation. He was so excited, but I was scared. I didn't know if I could handle another baby. Brittini wasn't even a year old yet. His excitement canceled out my fears. We were both changing, though. Sean still got very angry, and his new job caused him to see a lot of awful stuff, which made him even more bitter. His words were damaging me in ways I can't describe.

I was becoming so cold and closed off. I didn't realize that my actions caused Sean to feel like I didn't need him. Brittini was the only one who could soften my heart at all.

When I was three months pregnant, Sean and I got separated again. This was before there were cell phones and e-mails. I had no idea how to get ahold of him. It was a very ugly separation. During the last three months of my pregnancy, I didn't talk to or see Sean at all. On December 18, 1992, exactly one week before Christmas, I had another beautiful baby girl. What a gift! She was amazing in every way. I gave her the name Alysha Rae. For some reason, Brittini called the baby "Soappy" or "Soap." I think she might have been a little jealous of her new baby sister and thought that wasn't a nice name to call her. The funny thing is, as Alysha got older, she liked that nickname. We still call her Soappy or Soap to this day.

The night I had her, I was lying in my hospital bed all alone when my phone rang. It was Sean. He asked me how I was and congratulated me on the baby. He asked if he could come and see her and Brittini because he had Christmas gifts for them. I said yes but didn't feel much of anything. I was so focused on my new baby and Brittini that nothing else really mattered to me. When he came over a couple of days later, it touched my heart to see him holding our girls. We didn't say much to each other, and then he was gone.

Over the next couple of months, Sean started to come around more and more. He asked me to dinner one night, and I accepted the invitation. We talked so much, and he apologized for all his mistakes. He told me he never stopped loving me, and I believed him. He wanted to get back together. Part of me screamed no, but another part of me still loved him, and I wanted the girls to have their mom and dad. So again we got back together, and again we just slapped a Band-Aid over the wounds.

Although we loved each other, life was tough. We were still poor, didn't have any time for just each other, and were still dealing with issues of anger, bitterness, and insecurities from our past. When Brittini was two and Alysha was eleven months old, I found out I was pregnant again. Sean was not excited this time. He said we weren't financially ready for another child, and we weren't stable enough to bring another baby into our family. He asked me if

I would consider another abortion. I stared at him blankly. Did I hear him right? He couldn't be serious. We had a fight over this, which ended in my calling to make an appointment to end this pregnancy. The next day, I asked my mom to watch the girls, and I went to the mall. I just wanted to be alone. On the way there, a secular song was playing on the radio, and the words I heard said, "A hero lies in you." Something in my spirit jerked. I knew the Lord was telling me that He placed a hero in me and that He had special plans for this baby. I went back home and canceled my appointment. I was having this baby. I told Sean that night about my decision, expecting another fight. He was okay with it. God had been softening his heart too.

Looking back, I know another reason the Lord spoke to me was because He knew I couldn't handle another loss. He knew that my heart would have been shattered beyond repair. I can now see the Lord's hand guiding me when I didn't even realize it.

On February 14, 1994, when I was four months pregnant, Sean and I got separated yet again. Of all days…Valentine's Day! I was worried about what everyone would think and about how I was going to raise three kids on my own, but I knew God would help me. I did not deserve anything from Him, but I figured He cared about my children. They were innocent in all of this. I felt so inadequate. I couldn't even keep my husband happy. I was such a lousy human being. To everyone on the outside, I looked like this sweet, innocent girl. "Poor Tracey has had so many rough breaks. She's so nice." They couldn't see inside of me, though. I don't know why God gave me my children, but they were what made me feel special. I got to be their mom. And I was having another one.

When I went for a sonogram this time, I found out I was having a boy. A boy! I was so excited that I called Sean. I don't know why I did that, but, hey, I was pregnant, and my hormones were crazy. It had been a month since I talked to him. Surprisingly, he was thrilled with the news. And yet once again, we decided to get back together. And yet again, we slapped some more Band-Aids on our wounds.

Our marriage was decent but not good. We decided we were going to stick it out no matter what this time. Even though we weren't happy most of the time, we were miserable without each other. What a predicament! So we tried to make the best of it. Sean really was a good man with a good heart, but we had no idea how to handle everything life had thrown at us. Unfortunately, we took out our hurts and frustrations on each other.

On July 27, 1994, our son, Sean Scott, Jr., was born. He was handsome and big. He weighed eight pounds and thirteen ounces. Remember, I only weighed ninety-five pounds. So, to me, this was quite a large child. But our son, Seanny, was perfect nonetheless. Our family was complete. We decided I should have my tubes tied while I was in the hospital. If not, at the rate we were going, I would have ten kids by the time I was thirty years old. So here we were—Sean was twenty-four, and I was twenty-three—and we had three children. Brittini was three years old, Alysha was nineteen months old, and Seanny was a newborn. Talk about busy! We didn't plan any of our kids, and, yes, we tried multiple types of birth control, but I believe God had a special plan for each one of our kids and our family as a whole.

Chapter 2

Life was hard and busy for the next three years, but it had settled into a normal routine. The children were doing wonderfully. Each one was so smart, beautiful, and unique. Sean and I had our ups and downs, but we were determined to hang in there. I was working a part-time job for a Christian chiropractor to help make ends meet, while Sean was working as a policeman and doing any side job he could find. He detailed cars, mowed lawns, cut down trees—anything that was offered to him. Life had finally settled down.

Like all policemen, Sean has a difficult job. People have no idea what they go through and what they risk on a daily basis. Some of the incidents he went to both horrified and sickened me. I never worried about Sean, though; I just kept him covered in prayer. Sean had made a few arrests within the same family, and a lot of people were unhappy about it. These people had committed a lot of crimes. I was never told all the details; I just know that our lives were being threatened because of it. Sean was not the type to back off if there was an injustice, and I wouldn't want anything less from him. I remember, one night while he was working, they came and drove their truck through our yard, leaving tracks all over it. I guess they were trying to send a message. It angered us, but we refused to let fear rule our lives. I am sure Sean was more stressed about it than I was because I only knew a portion of what was really going on.

The kids were our pride and joy. We always celebrated their birthdays with big parties. Seanny's third birthday was no exception. We had about thirty-five people over to our house and celebrated all day long. We were all so tired when the day was finally over. The next morning when Seanny got out of bed, he was limping pretty severely. He probably fell at his party, and I had missed it. Sean thought I should take him to the doctor. He was concerned that it was possibly related to his hip, and if we wanted him to play sports someday, we shouldn't ignore it. So later that day, as Seanny and I sat in the exam room, the doctor informed me that Seanny just had a sprained ankle. It would heal in a few weeks, so he told me to just try to keep him calm and sitting as much as possible. Really? Keep an active three-year-old boy still? Obviously he wasn't a mother.

As the days went by, Seanny's leg just wasn't getting any better. Of course he was still playing and running around as much as he could. I hated to take him back to the doctor, knowing I hadn't kept him as still as possible. I could just hear the doctor say, "Sure, he's not getting any better if he's using it all the time. Did you hear what I told you the first visit?"

But after three weeks had gone by, I decided to make another appointment. Poor kid, there were times he was crawling to avoid using his leg.

So on August 26, 1997, I took Seanny back to our family doctor. Sean stayed at home with the girls. He told them he would play whiffle ball with them until I got back. As Seanny and I waited for the doctor to come in the exam room to see us, we joked and played around. The doctor came in and started to examine Seanny. He had a couple of small bruises on his leg. The doctor asked me how long they had been there. Was he serious? My kids and I always had cuts and bruises on us. We were all very active and sometimes clumsy. The doctor said he wanted to check his hemoglobin. He was concerned that Seanny might be anemic, which would cause his healing to take a lot longer. So the nurse came in, pricked his finger, and told us that the results would only take a few minutes. Seanny was sitting on my lap, and I was tickling him when the doctor came back in. I looked up at the doctor, and my heart momentarily stopped. The doctor had tears in his eyes. That couldn't be good. He proceeded to tell me that I needed to get Seanny to Children's Hospital immediately. I asked him what was wrong. Was it more a leg problem than his ankle? He couldn't answer me for a moment. Finally he said, "I think your son has leukemia. His blood counts are dangerously low."

The tears started rolling down his cheeks, and I just sat there motionless. There had to be some mistake. Seanny was just limping, that's all. I felt like there was an elephant sitting on my chest, and I was trying to see through a fog. As I stepped out of the room, all the office personnel were standing there, giving me this sympathetic look. They were so kind, but their words weren't sinking in. As we got in our car, I could feel tears in my eyes. Seanny asked me what was wrong, and I told him I was really mad at the devil right now. I had to stay in control. Breathe. Seanny needed me, and all my kids hated to see me upset. I dialed Sean's number. He answered the phone and asked me how the appointment went. With a shaky voice, I told him to find a sitter for the girls because we needed to get Seanny to Children's Hospital right away. He gave a laugh and said a sprained ankle couldn't be that big of an emergency.

I choked out, "The doctor thinks Seanny has leukemia."

I don't even remember if Sean said good-bye. I was driving home, and Seanny started singing "Jesus Loves Me."

Desperately I prayed, "Oh, Lord, please love my little boy. Please don't let him have leukemia. Let this all be a big mistake. Lord, I'll do anything… anything. Just take this away. Punish me, not my son. He doesn't deserve this."

I pulled into my driveway and took Seanny inside to see his sisters. I left them playing for a minute; I just had to get Seanny on the prayer chain. First I wanted to call my dad; he was always a rock in situations like this. He never overreacted. I hadn't really cried up until that point, but when I said the word "leukemia" to my dad, I got choked up and could feel the tears rolling down my cheeks. He offered to go with us, but I told him no. I said, "Let's wait until we're sure what we're dealing with."

Where was Sean? I hadn't seen him yet. We really needed to get going. His parents arrived to watch the girls. I found Sean out back standing by the garage, struggling to regain his composure. Without saying anything, we just got into the car and headed to the hospital. Although Pittsburgh was only about forty-five minutes from our house, we had no idea where we were going. I sat in the backseat with Seanny, just singing songs. We made a few wrong turns and ran into a lot of traffic, but about an hour and a half later, we were pulling into the hospital parking garage. Our doctor had called ahead to let them know we were coming, so they took us back to an exam room immediately. They quickly started drawing blood, and Seanny's face turned a dark-bluish color. What was happening? He looked worse than before we had gotten there. Weren't they supposed to be helping him? A nurse must have been able to read my expression, and she tried to explain what was going on. His blood counts were so low and bad that drawing blood was putting a huge strain on his body. It was necessary though. They needed to start testing it, and they needed to know what blood type he was. They said they knew he was going to need a transfusion before they even got the results. Sean and I both responded without hesitation that we would give him our blood. They said that would take too long. He was going to need a transfusion immediately. My mind started reeling with thoughts. What if the blood they gave him was infected with AIDS? That would be worse than leukemia. Should we allow them to do this to our son? As my mind was going from question to question, the results of his blood work arrived. All his blood counts were out of control. His platelets were so low that if he had fallen out in the yard earlier that day and gotten cut, he could have bled to death! His white blood cells were dangerously low. His hemoglobin was four. It should have been around twelve. They ordered a transfusion stat, saying he would die without it.

The doctor was so kind. He lent Sean his personal phone to make any calls necessary. Sean was due at work for the 11:00 p.m. to 7:00 a.m. shift. Sean took the phone and left the room. I sat on the bed with Seanny while they hooked him up to various machines. The doctor told me they were almost certain Seanny had leukemia but wouldn't know for sure until they did a bone marrow test in the morning. They called in an oncologist to meet with us and explain what was going on. I didn't even know what an oncologist was. They told me it was a cancer doctor, a specialist in that field. Oh, maybe I had heard that before. They told us we were lucky to get the doctor that was on call because she was one of the best in the country. They said there was a waiting list of patients that wanted her. I wasn't feeling so lucky, but I was thankful to know Seanny would be in good hands. The doctor commented to me how strong I was and how impressed he was with how I was handling everything. He couldn't see inside of me. Sure, I was laughing and playing with Seanny. He needed me. If I showed fear…he would be scared. I could not lose my son, my only son, my baby.

The only other person I ever knew who had leukemia was my grandpap, and he died from it. Great, just great. Now it was my fault that Seanny had this. It came from my side of the family, and I must have passed on the gene or something.

Sean returned to the room just as the oncologist was coming in. She explained the situation to us. Seanny was showing every sign of having leukemia. Nothing would be sure until the bone marrow test. If he had leukemia, he would be in the hospital for one to two months. During that time, he would need multiple transfusions of blood and platelets. They would find a good treatment plan and start immediately. Although they tried to be hopeful, they made it clear that there were no guarantees. Cancer is unpredictable. For now, he would be admitted to the hospital and assigned a room.

We got to Seanny's room very late that night. It was an isolation room. Seanny had to be in a very clean, sterile environment. His immune system was not working. Oh, well, at least we had some privacy. Sean kissed us good-bye and said he'd see us the next day. There was absolutely no way I was leaving my son alone, not even for a minute. I was not going back to my job. I was staying right there. I didn't know how we would afford our bills, but I didn't care. Was I really just fretting and worrying about money earlier that day? That seemed so petty in the light of things now. I felt weak. Where was Sean when I needed him? I could have really used a shoulder and a hug right about then.

A nurse came in to put an IV in Seanny. She hooked the fluids to it and left. As I sat next to my son, he started to doze. I was holding his hand and thought something was wrong. I looked at his hand and arm and saw a lump the size of a golf ball on his tiny forearm. I buzzed for a nurse, thinking, *Oh, my goodness, his arm is going to explode.*

When the nurse came in, she wasn't overly concerned. She adjusted his IV and said she'd be back in a little while. What was common to her wasn't to me. The lump slowly started to go down.

Seanny fell asleep quickly. I wasn't so fortunate. I had been lying in bed with him and quietly got up. My thoughts turned to my girls. I had never been away from them except to give birth. They needed me, too. I couldn't be in two places at once. Sigh. Too much to think about. I found a Bible, went to a corner of the room, and found a nightlight to read by.

I was raised in a Christian home, got saved at a young age, and grew up respecting God. I loved God, and Jesus was my Lord, but I didn't really know God on a deep, personal level. My dad taught us Bible trivia like no other. We could tell you details about the Bible that some preachers didn't know! My mom was raised in a Christian family, but my dad didn't come to know Jesus until he was thirty. The church I attended while growing up taught salvation but not much else. I didn't expect anything from God while still on this earth. It was okay to make requests to God, but the answer you wanted could go either way. God was sovereign, and He could choose to give any answer He wanted. If you were good enough, you had a better chance at getting your prayers answered. But be careful what you ask for; you might not like what you get. Besides, God teaches you something through suffering. If you handle it right, He gets glory from it. At least that's what I had been taught.

I started talking to God. "Lord, how can this be Your will for my child? I don't want his healing to come through death. Lord, I love him too much."

I closed my eyes, and in my spirit, I heard a voice whisper, "I love him more than you do."

My eyes shot wide open. It was the Lord; something in me just knew. His voice was tender, caring, strong, and loving. It was not the voice I was used to hearing. I believed what He said in my mind but not in my heart. I knew God was capable of loving more than I could, but this was my only son. His heart couldn't be nearly as invested as mine.

I closed my eyes again, and the Lord whispered, "I know how your heart breaks to see your son hurting. I went through it with my Son, too. I love Seanny more than you do."

And His words sunk deep into my heart. He was the Voice of Truth. All my life I heard a voice telling me I got what I deserved and that nobody truly loved me. I had always believed that love was conditional. This voice, though…oh, this voice. Something in me broke. I knew it was God, and He cared enough to come and comfort me. He came to be at my side in my greatest time of need when I was alone.

I started talking back to Him. "Lord, this can't be from you. Putting a deadly disease on a little child. Why would You do this? Please tell me. I'll believe anything you tell me."

"My child, this isn't from Me. There is an enemy out there that seeks to destroy. If you'll trust Me, really trust Me, I'll turn this around. We are going to reach thousands upon thousands with this testimony."

Did I hear Him right? I was not a very outgoing person, not to mention a not-so-good speaker. He must have been talking about the rest of the family. I continued to listen.

"First, you cannot let any negative words around Seanny."

I had absolutely no idea why He said this, but I replied, "Okay, God. I'll do whatever You tell me."

I was desperate.

I didn't have any paper with me at the hospital, so I found a brown paper towel and a pen. I wrote boldly on the paper towel, "Please no negative words past this door. God's working a miracle inside!"

I don't know why I wrote this, but I did. Then I found some medical tape and hung my paper-towel sign on the door.

I asked the Lord to show me scriptures from the Bible that I needed to hear. I opened up my Bible to Leviticus 26. This chapter talks about the rewards for obedience and the punishment for disobedience. I thought, *Wow, these rewards are awesome. I'll be obedient.*

I just put a burden on myself that I wouldn't be able to carry. Being obedient sounds easy, but it is impossible. I unknowingly made a way to put more guilt on myself. Little did I know it at the time, but I was listening to two different voices. I was hearing God in my spirit but also listening to the voice of lies. It wouldn't be for a while that God explained the differences between the old and new covenants to me. I had read the scripture many times when Jesus said, "My sheep know My voice and they follow me." I didn't know my God well enough to always recognize His voice from the enemy's.

Thankfully, God was more than willing to work with me from where I was. He had to take me baby step by baby step.

I was finally getting tired. It was well after midnight, and I knew they needed us up early. I lay down in bed next to Seanny. Thankfully, we were both small enough to fit in that hospital bed together; otherwise, I would have had to sleep on a chair—a plastic, vinyl one at that. I had no idea that someone would be in every thirty to forty-five minutes to check on him. How in the world do people get rest in a hospital?! That was the most broken night's sleep I had ever had.

Chapter 3

Early the next morning, a crew of medical staff came in our room to perform a bone marrow test on Seanny. They told me they would take a long needle and push it into Seanny's hip until it reached his bone marrow. They told me the bone marrow is the deepest part of your physical body. First they would give Seanny a twilight drug. They asked me if I wanted to stay in the room, and I said of course. Where else would I want to be? Outside in the hall, wondering what in the world was going on with my son? They told me if I could handle it, I could lie on the bed and hold Seanny still while they performed the test. I would make myself handle it.

When they were ready, I got on the bed, holding Seanny on top of me. I wrapped my arms and legs around him, knowing it was very important that he not move. Although I couldn't directly see what they were doing, I could see enough. They were really pushing that incredibly long needle into him. He moaned a little but was a real trooper through it all. The nurse practitioner was so sympathetic; she even had tears in her eyes by the time it was through. I was complimented on how well I did and was told I could do it again next time. Next time?! How many times would we have to do this? Sometimes it is a good thing we can't see into the future and know the answers to all of our questions. It would be too overwhelming.

We were told that we would have the results later that afternoon. During the day, Seanny lay in bed a lot and watched television. He started getting bouquets of balloons and cookies. The phone seemed to ring nonstop. He hadn't even been in the hospital fifteen hours yet. By this time, Seanny was on his third transfusion. His leg cramps were increasing in severity and frequency. Soon…we would have some answers.

Sean arrived back at the hospital. Together we tried to keep Seanny entertained. The clock was ticking ever so slowly. Finally, the doctor knocked on our door. She came in and took a seat. I already knew what she was going to say. I had been preparing all day for this. She looked directly at us and said, "Your son has leukemia ALL."

Just like that, our world came tumbling down. Surprisingly, neither Sean nor I fainted.

"What exactly is that?" I heard myself ask.

"ALL stands for acute lymphoblastic leukemia. It is a cancer of the white blood cells. It crowds out the bone marrow, preventing it from working normally. It invades the blood quickly and can spread into the lymph nodes, spleen, brain, and spine. We will have to do spinals frequently to make sure the cancer hasn't moved into his spine. Right now his spleen is very enlarged, but we can take it out if necessary. His bone marrow is ninety-two percent leukemic. We will have to start treatment immediately. The chemotherapy plan consists of three and a half years of treatments. Do you have any questions?"

Did she really just say three and a half years? That seemed like a life sentence.

"Was he born with it?" I asked.

"There's no way to tell for sure but probably not," she responded.

"Are you sure he really has it? Could this be a mistake?" I heard my husband ask.

"There is no mistake. I know this is a lot to take in, and I have a lot of material for you to read. Unfortunately, time is not on our side. We need you both to sign some papers giving us permission to start chemotherapy."

"One more question for now. Why does Seanny's leg hurt so much?"

I had to know if this was related in any way.

"His bone marrow has so much leukemia; it's causing him the pain. We can give him medication when it happens. We'll be back shortly to get your answer and signatures," she said.

She was very patient and compassionate, but this was routine to her. It was anything but normal to us.

Sean looked at me and said, "What if he doesn't really have it? What if we sign these papers, and he doesn't really have it? What if this is some kind of experiment? Do we want to chance it?"

"What if he does have it, and we don't sign those papers? According to them, he'll die without treatment. Do you want to chance it? I believe they are right," I replied, trying to be the voice of reason.

"What choice do we have? This is all just crazy. I'll sign," Sean said softly with defeat in his voice.

Silently I prayed, "God, you told me last night that if I trusted You, everything would be okay. I have no one else to rely on here. The doctor is a human just like me. She has limitations. You don't. Guide us, Lord. Work with us where we are at."

They came back in shortly with forms for us to read and sign. We didn't understand everything we were reading but got the general idea of what it was saying. Sean signed the papers. Then I signed them. I had never, and haven't since, signed something of greater significance. We just gave permission to put highly toxic chemicals into our son's body. I knew chemotherapy could attack and destroy the good cells along with the bad. With a quick stroke of the pen, we changed our son's life forever.

Sean went home shortly after this. I called the girls to see how they were doing. They were with Pappy and Grandma Kelley. Pappy always played and made sure they had a fun time, and Grandma was always cooking and baking for them. Good, they were happy and content. I missed them so much. My heart was being tugged on in so many directions.

The nurses were coming into our room every couple of hours to take his blood so that they would know what his counts were. Nothing was stabilizing. That night as Seanny fell asleep, one of the nurses brought in the crash cart. She told me that Seanny's calcium count was so low that there was a very good chance his heart might stop or be put under heavy stress. They already had him hooked up to a heart monitor.

I had to catch my breath. Did she really say my son's heart might stop?

Since I knew I would not be sleeping after hearing that news, I got out the Bible. I asked the Lord to please reveal to me what I was reading. I didn't want it to be just trivial facts any longer. I wanted to get to know God more deeply and understand the truth. It was going to be a long night, and I planned on getting to know my God. I now fully understood that the reason I didn't know what to expect from God was because I didn't really know Him. That was about to change.

It seemed like every scripture I flipped to was about healing. First I read in Isaiah 53:5, "He was pierced for our transgressions, He was crushed for our iniquities, the punishment that brought us peace was upon Him, and by His stripes we are healed."

Then I came across Psalm 103:5: "Praise the Lord, O my soul; all my inmost being praise His holy name. Praise the Lord, O my soul, and forget not all His benefits—who forgives all your sins and heals all your diseases…"

Next I read in Psalm 107:19 and 20, "Then they cried out to the Lord in their trouble, and He saved them from their distress. He sent forth His word and healed them; He rescued them from the grave."

Psalm 188:17 states, "I will not die but live, and will proclaim what the Lord has done."

On and on and on, these verses kept coming. I never realized how important our physical health was to God. I thought He was only concerned with our spirits. I was beginning to see that when you are hungry for the truth, God will feed you.

When I read James 1:5–8, it pulled it all together. "If any of you lacks wisdom, he should ask God, who gives generously to all without finding fault, and it will be given to him. But when he asks, he must believe and not doubt, because he who doubts is like a wave of the sea, blown and tossed by the wind. That man should not think he will receive anything from the Lord; he is a double-minded man, unstable in all he does."

I just had to trust God. I could not mix the truth with lies. I could not mix the truth with facts. I could not mix the truth with doubt. I needed to take God at His word, period. I decided right then and there that I was always going to believe God. I mean if you could not trust God, who could you trust?

After reading for a couple of hours, I closed my eyes and thanked God for all He was teaching me. I felt God telling me to give Seanny completely to Him. I mentally pictured myself carrying my precious baby boy and laying him at the foot of the cross. I could see Jesus's blood dripping down onto my boy. Then I could see Jesus in Heaven, holding Seanny against His chest. He was loving my son as if he were the only human being ever. I then knew that… Jesus did love my son more than I did.

That night, not only did I realize that God was completely trustworthy, but I was falling in love with Him. I could feel God chipping away at my stone heart. No matter what happened, I was sold out to God. Nothing on this earth was going to change my feelings toward Jesus.

The sun was shining through the window early in the morning. I could hear the sound of birds chirping. They never had to use the crash cart. I breathed a deep sigh of relief. Thank you, Jesus. Thank you, Jesus. Thank you, Jesus.

As I was stretching and waking up, a nurse practitioner came into our room. She told me Seanny's calcium level was stabilizing and under control, but now his potassium level had dropped drastically. They were concerned he might go into kidney failure. They wanted to put a shunt in him as soon as possible for dialysis. They were scheduling surgery for that morning. I was told not to let him eat anything until the operation was completed. I went into the bathroom, where Seanny couldn't see me, to pray.

"Lord, thank you so much for getting his calcium under control. I know that you are working a miracle even if Seanny has to have this surgery. But, Lord, please spare him from this. He's been through so much already. Thank you, Jesus, for taking care of this situation."

I decided if Seanny couldn't eat, then I wouldn't either. His surgery was scheduled for late morning. We colored, watched TV, and played with his cars—anything to keep our minds off our growling stomachs. By 1:00 p.m., I buzzed for a nurse. I asked her why Seanny had not been taken down for surgery yet. She said the operating room was overbooked, but it shouldn't be much longer. I knew the delay wasn't intentional, but we were hungry. By 2:30 p.m., another nurse came in to tell us they would be taking him down to the OR soon.

I don't know why I said it, but I heard myself asking, "Could you please do a blood count again before he goes down?"

Shockingly, the nurse said they would. About half an hour later, the nurse came into the room and told me his surgery was canceled. His potassium level was within normal range. I had just witnessed a miracle. My heart was filled with gratitude for what God had done. And now we could eat!

Seanny had to have another blood transfusion that day. He always perked up afterward. A social worker came to visit late in the afternoon. He gave me information to read and asked me if I would like to be connected with a support group.

I told him, "No, thank you. God is all the support I need."

I was also thinking that I didn't want to go to a group where people were depressed and crying about how awfully cancer had affected their lives. I was beginning to see how important it was to guard my thoughts and what I heard. Then they proceeded to tell us maybe Sean and I should go to counseling. The divorce rate is very high for couples going through what we were. That's just what we needed to hear. We declined.

We were starting to get a lot of visitors, mostly family. I look back and find it funny that I had to encourage them. They would walk into the room, see Seanny hooked up to multiple machines, and start crying. They all cared so deeply, it touched my heart. I boldly told them all that Seanny would be healed. I know everyone, including the medical staff, thought I was either losing it or in complete denial. I had such peace that I would greet everyone with a smile and kind words. Little did I know that people were asking Sean if I was really okay. Sean later told me he was so concerned that if Seanny didn't make it, I would have a breakdown or something. He was preparing himself for the worst, but he didn't think I was aware of what was really happening.

I was there 24/7. I heard every report, read all the information they gave me, and watched every test taken. I was immersed in reality, more than anyone, but I trusted God and His word. And He was giving me His peace that passed all understanding.

My dad came to visit me every day. The kids called him Pappy Kelley. He was the strong one of the family. He never cried or said anything negative about the situation. He would come straight from work in his mailman uniform and visit with us. He always asked if we needed food. My parents didn't have much either, so I knew what a sacrifice my dad was making to come see us every day and to buy us food occasionally. He never complained, though. He always acted like it was his pleasure to get to spend some time with us.

That evening, Seanny started crying because of his leg. His little body shook from the pain. I buzzed the nurse, and when she entered the room, I asked her to please get him something for it. I cradled my little boy and started to sing him one of our favorite Sunday school songs:

"Love Him, love Him in the morning when you see the sun arising.
Love Him in the evening 'cause He took you through the day.
And in the in-between time when you feel the pressure coming,
Remember that He loves you and He promises to stay."

As I sang, Seanny started to calm down. By the time the nurse came back, he was asleep. She was amazed that the pain had left him so quickly and without medication—and so was I.

Other than being woken up every couple of hours, we had a good night's sleep. We were starting to fall into a routine there. They had started Seanny's chemo and would give him transfusions when needed. The first thing in the morning, Seanny would get to look at a menu and pick his meals for the day. Since money was so tight, I would only order lunch. Seanny's was paid for through our insurance, but I would have to pay for any meal I ate. Mail time was always exciting. People found out that Seanny liked cars just like his dad. Many of the cards would have a Matchbox car included. Seanny received over a hundred cards and letters in the first week and at least thirty little cars. Gifts were in abundance too: tool sets, coloring books, movies, blankets, and money, just to name a few. It was comforting to know that so many people cared about and were praying for our family.

Chapter 4

After a few days, the doctor told us they were going to surgically put a mediport into Seanny's chest. She explained this was a device that would be implanted to accept an IV during his treatments. The doctor informed us that between the chemicals and constant insertion of a needle into his arm over the next three and a half years, his veins would be damaged. The mediport would be less painful to access each time, and it would keep his veins from being harmed.

As they wheeled him down for surgery, Sean and I walked beside our baby. I was joking around with him, trying to make him laugh. As we got to the operating room, they told us to go to the waiting room. What? I begged them to let me go with my son. They said this was a more serious surgery, and I wasn't allowed in. I quickly gave him a hug and a kiss and told him I would see him soon. I had to get away quickly; I could feel myself holding back the tears. I wanted—no, needed—to be with Seanny. This was my hardest day yet. When I sat down next to my husband in the waiting room, I asked him to please hold me. I always kept a wall up, acting like I didn't need anyone, but for the first time, I felt shaky. Sean looked at me and said no.

Did I hear him right? In my greatest time of need, did he really just say that? I looked at him coldly and said, "Are you serious?"

He said, "I am tired of everyone thinking you're the strong one. I'm tired of hearing how good and in control you are and how lucky I am. You have no idea."

I have no idea of what? What was he talking about? Over the next fifteen minutes, Sean's words shocked and hurt me. I put my wall back up unbelievably quickly. I went numb. Finally we both just got silent. Silence was always my first defense.

I didn't realize how much Sean was struggling. I figured since he got to go to work, he wasn't thinking about Seanny 100 percent of the time. He wasn't surrounded by doctors, nurses, reports, and tests like I was. He didn't watch his son go through so much pain and torture. Okay, so maybe it wasn't torture, but he had so many needles and tubes stuck in him daily. Sean was fortunate that he didn't have those images stuck in his mind. That is what I thought. But the truth was, besides dealing with the pressures of his job, he was worried about his son nonstop. So many negative thoughts crossed his mind constantly. He was worried that his son was dying. He didn't want to live life without him. Instead of talking to each other about all of this, we hurt each other. Our communicating skills with each other really could use some improvement.

When the nurse came into the waiting room, she told us Seanny's surgery went well. They were going to be taking him back to his room, even though he was still a little groggy. Thank God. I couldn't wait to see my son. As we walked back to Seanny's room, my attention was 100 percent on him. I would not even make eye contact with my husband. Seanny had such a huge bandage on his little chest. But the surgery was over. What a relief.

I was going over in my head what I was going to say to Sean when we got back to the room, but when we opened the door, two of our very close friends were sitting there waiting for us. It was so good to see them, but I wanted to be alone with my husband. We got Seanny back in bed, and he fell asleep almost instantly. They had brought dinner for all of us, so we sat in our vinyl hospital chairs and ate together. I could feel myself relaxing. After a couple of hours, they said they should go. Sean said it was time for him to leave also, so he'd walk out with them. I knew Sean did not want to be alone with me. He had known me long enough to know what I was thinking.

After he left, I started to talk to God. My heart was hurting so badly. How could my husband treat me this way? I rarely asked him to be there for me, but the very few times I have, he's hurt me. I could feel my heart getting hard again. I would shut off my feelings to survive. God gently told me that Sean was trying to handle everything on his own and with his own power.

Sean was finding out it wasn't enough. And he always resorted to anger as the first emotion he let himself feel. We were raised so differently. I was taught to bottle things up and not talk about them. Sean was raised to get angry and let everything out. God gently reminded me that both ways were damaging to our marriage. God told me that although I could not tell, Sean leaned on me. When I had a hard time, he couldn't handle it. Down deep, it scared him. So with our friends being in our room when we got there, Sean leaving before we got to be alone, and God talking to me, I let the whole ugly incident go. How did I do that? By putting another Band-Aid on it, of course. I thought I understood the situation better then, so I would just bury it. I never really considered talking about it and truly fixing anything. By this time in our marriage, I believe we were on about our fourth box of Band-Aids.

The next morning, when Seanny woke up, he was bruised from his neck to his belly from the surgery. The mediport was raised clearly above the skin level, and you could see the lines running in his neck from it. It would be a constant reminder of what we were dealing with every time we looked at him. But he was still so beautiful and precious. He was handling everything so incredibly well.

I had explained to Seanny the first day we were there that the doctors and nurses were only trying to help him. If they hurt him in the process, they didn't mean to. I told him to always be grateful for their help. So every time a doctor or nurse worked on him, he would always say thank you. Even when they made him cry, he would still thank them when they were through. I was so proud of him.

Seanny continued to have leg pain the first couple of weeks. The pain would get so intense that his little body would quiver. Every time we called for pain medicine, we would sing until they got there. And by the time they arrived, his pain would be gone. They never had to give him pain medicine. No one, including me, had any idea what was going on. They said I must have a magic voice. I knew that was not the case. Singing was definitely not my gift either.

Seanny's taste buds dulling was one of the many side effects of his chemo. Late one night, Seanny was hungry but didn't know what for. The nurse on duty said he was going down to the kitchen to get something for him that he thought Seanny would like. He returned about half an hour later with some hot wings. Seanny cautiously took a bite of one then another.

He said, "Boy, these are good" as sauce dripped down his face.

And so started Seanny's love for the food. Every night that nurse was on duty, he would go to the kitchen and get some for Seanny. I thought that was so nice; he didn't have to do it. He never charged us a penny and acted like it was his pleasure to do it. God brought so many special "angels" into our lives.

Even though we got visitors and tons of mail, the days were long when it was just Seanny and me. He wasn't allowed to leave his room, so what we could do was very limited. He had brought the movie *Space Jam* from home, and we watched it at least three times a day. One nurse commented that we were watching it too much, but what else was there to do? We colored for hours a day, played cars, took naps, read books, ate, and prayed for people, which still left a lot of time on our hands. Seanny never complained, but he would get restless at times.

The hospital had a "sibs" day about a week after we got there. This is when siblings got to go on a tour of the hospital and see what every day was like for their brother or sister. Brittini and Alysha had such a good time. It was good to see all of them together again. The girls were doing great. They were mostly staying with my parents, and Pappy was always making up games for them, taping them as they made their own movies, or playing sports with them. So the girls felt like they were on a mini vacation. I was so glad to be able to hug them and snuggle with them for a few hours. The day ended way too soon.

The nurses started to bring in pills for Seanny to take as part of his chemo. This was an area of stress because no matter how hard Seanny tried, he could not seem to get those pills down.

After a few days, one of the nurses sternly said to Seanny, "You need to learn to get these pills down if you ever want to get out of the hospital. You won't get to go home until you learn to swallow pills."

My anger and protective streak flashed on high instantly. I asked if I could see her in the hall.

When we got there, I told her, "My son is only three years old, and he is trying extremely hard to do everything you ask of him. His world has been flipped upside down. He can't wait to get out of the hospital. You will never talk to my son that way again or threaten him with never going home. I appreciate the job you are doing, but I will not allow you to speak that way to him."

We really did have wonderful doctors and nurses, though. The majority went out of their way to make a bad situation bearable. I remember one time a worker asked Seanny if he knew what cancer was.

Seanny said, "It makes me sick. It's not a big deal, though. God is working a miracle. But if I die, I just get to go see Jesus."

I could not believe what I was hearing. No one said anything about dying or being extremely sick around Seanny; I would not allow it. Yet here he was, talking like a very mature Christian, putting things into perspective better than any adult. I was just overwhelmed.

Chapter 5

Days passed by methodically. Each day brought blessings and miracles, and each day had its trials and obstacles. One evening, I was sitting next to Seanny's bed while he took a nap. I was reading and chewing ice. I felt a weird crunch in my head and realized that I broke one of my molars in half. I never had anything like that happen before. Great, just great. I didn't have time for this. Thankfully, it didn't hurt much at all. I decided to ignore it and someday in the faraway future get it taken care of. Such inconveniences!

Another hard day for me happened a little over a week after we had been in the hospital. Brittini was having her first day of first grade. Oh, how I wanted to be there, but my place was with Seanny for the time being. It broke my heart. I asked Sean to have her call me before she left that morning. My dad went to our house to take a video of Brittini and Alysha so I could at least witness the day. That call and those pictures are priceless to me. I prayed for her constantly throughout the day.

Brittini was always a very sweet, outgoing girl. Her first-grade teacher told me a story about my daughter's first week in first grade. The teacher was having a bad day. She wasn't being overly patient with the students. She was short with Brittini. A few minutes later, Brittini walked up to her desk, struggling not to cry, and told her, "I am sorry you're having a bad day. I am praying for you. Jesus loves you."

The teacher later told me she was pregnant and having a rough day. As she was with some of the other teachers, she told them the story of Brittini. One of the teachers replied, "Wow, it's hard to believe she is so thoughtful and kind with everything going on in her life."

Brittini's teacher quickly asked, "What do you mean?"

The other teacher said, "Well, her younger brother is in the hospital fighting for his life against cancer, and she doesn't get to see her mom very much."

Brittini's teacher said this news made her cry and humbled her. She said it's been a reminder over the years that you never know what a child is facing and going through. It really blessed my heart to know God's love was shining through my children.

I missed my girls so much. I got to see them every few days and talked to them on the phone as much as we could afford. This was before cell phones and calling plans, and these were long-distance calls. I remember buying stuffed horses for them from the gift shop and mailing them to them. To this day, they still have them and said it is one of their favorite gifts ever.

I was encouraged by a lot of the medical staff to go home for a day. They said it wasn't good for me to never leave the hospital for a break. What kind of relaxing break would I have if I wasn't with Seanny? I couldn't imagine how alone he would feel without me there. The children who didn't have anyone to stay with them had beds that looked like big, enclosed cribs. This was so they wouldn't fall or get out of bed unsupervised. I didn't want Seanny to think he was in jail. They talked to Sean and told him to convince me to take a break. There was no way I was leaving. They could not have even physically removed me. Sean knew to let it go. I was one of the most stubborn people he knew. I might have been a skinny little lady, but inside I was a fiercely ferocious mother.

When Seanny would take a nap or go to sleep for the night, I would get out the Bible and read. God was constantly teaching me. I read in 1 Samuel 16:23 how David would play music for King Saul when an evil spirit tormented him. Then he would feel better. Then I read in Psalm 22 that God inhabits the praises of His people. Then it clicked! When I would sing praise songs to God while Seanny was hurting, the pain would just leave. I saw it happen multiple times. It had nothing to do with my voice and everything to do with praising and focusing on God.

God had told me the first night to guard my words, especially around Seanny. I had no idea why; it must have had something to do with positive thinking. Then God started showing me the power in words, especially when they lined up with His word. Psalm 107:2 says, "Let the redeemed of the Lord *say* so." Proverbs 18:21 states, "Death and life are in the power of the *tongue*." And one of my favorites is from Mark 11:23: "Truly I tell you, if anyone *says* to this mountain, 'Go throw yourself into the sea,' and does not doubt in his heart but believes that what they *say* will happen, it will be done for them."

It's funny how God had to get me alone, away from theology and religion, to teach me the truth. I don't believe anyone ever intentionally misguided me, but I was taught many things that were not in the Bible. The more I read His word, the more I understood Him. The more I understood Him, the closer I wanted to get. It was a wonderful circle.

When I read John 10:10, "The thief [which is the devil] comes to steal, kill, and destroy. I [Jesus] have come to give life, and to give it abundantly," I realized God only gives us good things. I saw how God got blamed for a lot of bad that happens on the earth. Some might think, *Well, He's God. He could at least stop it. This bad stuff must be His will.* This is such an awful lie that people put on God. If that's the case, why isn't everyone saved? It is God's will that none perish. The reason is because God gave us free will; He didn't make us robots. God is a gentleman; He doesn't force His ways or will on anyone.

God is good, and the more I got to know Him, the more trustworthy I found Him to be. God told me how it hurt His heart not to be trusted or believed. I could see Him working mightily in my family's lives. I could see my prayers getting answered. I remembered the day a nurse brought Seanny in a cup full of pills, and he just started popping them in his mouth and swallowing them. After days of trying, when I finally asked God to help in this area, he had no more problems.

As I said, days seem long when you are stuck in a hospital. One evening, we were listening to some slow ballads, and Seanny asked if he could dance with me. I picked him up carefully so I wouldn't pull on any of his wires or tubes and started swaying back and forth. He put his head on my shoulder. Some of the lyrics to the song were: "I would cross the ocean for you, I would go and bring you the moon; I will be your hero, your strength, everything you need." Oh, I loved this little boy so much, beyond what words can describe. A couple of negative thoughts crept into my head, thoughts like, *Enjoy this now because you'll never get the chance to dance with him as a teenager or an adult.* By then I was starting to recognize the voice of lies, the voice of fear. I had to immediately replace those thoughts with the word of God.

I told Seanny, "I love dancing with you. When you get older, we'll still do this together."

I was speaking words of life, words that spoke of Seanny being alive for a long time.

When we had been in the hospital for almost three weeks, the doctor came into our room and said, "Seanny's counts have been stabilizing, and the chemo is going well. We are going to let you go home tomorrow."

This was too good to be true. I was so excited. I called Sean and told him the good news. I think he was even more excited than I was. He never said it, but I think he was glad to have me coming home to take care of the laundry, dishes, bills, and the girls. That was fine by me; I wanted life to go back to normal.

That evening, Sean showed up at the hospital and told me he was spending the night there with Seanny and me. That way he could take us home first thing in the morning. I told him I usually slept in the bed with Seanny, but there was a vinyl chair that would lay flat that he could sleep on. Seanny went to sleep early that night, so Sean and I got to really talk for the first time in weeks. He told me how some of our friends and neighbors had organized a car wash to raise money for Seanny. They raised around four hundred dollars. I was amazed that people would do something so nice for us.

It felt good to have Sean there with me. It was as if I wasn't on duty by myself for a change. I could actually feel myself relax. Sean leaned over and kissed me. I gave him an ornery, flirtatious smile and told him that he'd better control himself.

He said, "What if I don't want to?"

I proceeded to tell him that nurses and doctors come in and out of the room frequently and unexpectedly.

He said, "I don't care. I have missed you so much."

I have to admit I missed him too.

So there we were, two very young adults with the weight of the world on our shoulders but acting like carefree teenagers. Although, looking back, I think we were crazy, it was a wonderful night. Smile.

Seanny was discharged early the next morning. They gave us a list of dos and don'ts that would take me a while to memorize: Make sure he takes all his medicines as directed. Don't let him eat much salt. Don't allow him around anyone who is sick. Make sure all visitors wash their hands when entering your house. Don't use public bathrooms. Don't use public water fountains. When his counts are low, keep him isolated as much as possible. Don't let him stay out in the sun for long. Make sure all the fruits and vegetables are washed thoroughly before allowing him to touch them. Do not allow him around children who have had live vaccinations. On and on and on the list went. I didn't mind, though; we were getting to go home. It took Sean at least five trips to get all the cards, presents, and balloons loaded up into our Suburban. Then the doctor starting writing prescriptions that Seanny would need to take at home. She asked if he needed liquids or pills. Really? The impatient nurse never told us that was an option. Being able to take the liquid form of his medicines would have been a lot easier. I was glad that he learned to swallow pills, though. Oh, well. Finally, we got to leave with him. It was so good to step outside the hospital. I felt like we had crossed a major milestone. Like I said earlier, it's a good thing we can't always see what the future holds.

On the way home, Sean asked me if we could stop at our friend's gas station that was close to our house. I told him that was fine. When we got there, I saw the owner's son, who was around twenty years old. His head was shaved bald. Sean asked him what happened because as long as we had known him, he always had a lot of hair. He said he didn't want Seanny to feel alone when his hair started to fall out. I was so deeply touched by his gesture. To know how much people cared made such a difference.

When we pulled into our driveway, I thought, *There truly is no place like home.* I walked into the door and immediately gave Alysha Rae a hug. I didn't want to let go. I missed her so much. Seanny wanted to eat immediately. I didn't realize the steroids he was on would make him feel hungry almost constantly. This was going to be a bit of a problem. Cooking wasn't my gift either. I could fix a few things, but Seanny wanted to eat eight times a day. Thankfully, people from our church started bringing us dinner. This lasted for over two weeks, which was a huge blessing to me. Now I only had to be concerned about seven meals a day.

When Brittini got off the school bus that afternoon, she saw me and came running to the porch. I swept her up in a big bear hug and twirled her around. She started talking, and I don't think she quit for at least an hour. I wanted to hear everything Brittini and Alysha had to say. I had missed them so much.

After a full day of catching up, I took the girls to bed and tucked them in. I then took Seanny to bed and tucked him in. As I walked to my own bedroom down the hall, I started wondering if I could hear Seanny from my room if he needed anything. What if his counts dropped during the night, and I wasn't next to him to notice? I didn't sleep well that first night at home. I got up at least once an hour to check on him. I would kneel next to his bed and stare at his chest to make sure it was going up and down with his breathing. I didn't realize how much I came to trust in the machines he was hooked up to in the hospital. If anything was wrong with Seanny, they would beep and alert the nurses if there was a problem. Of course I didn't tell anyone about my fear. Sean worked midnights, so he wasn't home to notice. He had no idea how protective I had become.

The next morning, I got up early to take Seanny to Children's Hospital Outpatient Oncology Clinic. I had to leave two hours before our appointment time because I knew I would hit rush-hour traffic. He had to get his blood counts checked and receive his chemotherapy intravenously. We walked into the clinic and were surprised at how many children were there. You sure couldn't feel sorry for yourself as you looked around the room. There were so many children with so many types of cancer. I was stunned. I met a child who was blind from a tumor pushing on his brain. I saw children whose legs were so swollen they couldn't walk. I saw a girl whose arm had been amputated. Most of the kids were bald. A lot of them were wearing masks because their immune systems were so weak they had to keep out the germs. Oh, how my heart ached for each one of them and their parents. I felt a crushing sadness pushing on my heart. I put on a smile and started making cheerful chitchat with Seanny and the other children. I didn't want Seanny to be scared, and I didn't want to make those children feel different.

When Seanny was called back to get weighed and have his blood pressure taken, I went with him. We were then escorted to a treatment room, where we met a nurse who would be working with him for the duration of his treatments. She was so nice and cheerful, thank God. It made both Seanny and me relax. She explained she would put a needle into Seanny's chest to access his mediport. She said it would be a little pinch. Seanny flinched as he got jabbed but didn't cry or get upset. She said she would be drawing blood from his port and send it to the lab down the hall. Once they saw that his counts were decent, they would put the chemo into his mediport. Unfortunately, she couldn't get anything to go in or out of his mediport. She tried and tried. She then had to insert a needle into his arm to perform the procedures. I was a little nervous. I asked her why his mediport wasn't working, and she said it happens sometimes. He needed to come back two more times that week for his chemotherapy, so she said she would try it again next time. If they couldn't get it to work properly within a week, they would have to do surgery to put a new one in. Sigh. Really? Why couldn't it just work like it was supposed to?

His counts were a little low but not enough to need any transfusions. At least that was good. They put his chemo into an IV with a slow drip. We were there for a few hours by the time he was done. On the way home, we stopped to eat. Seanny was so hungry, poor thing. We picked up Alysha from my mom's and then went home to get Brittini off the school bus.

My day had started at 5:30 a.m., and it was around five o'clock in the afternoon. I sighed a sigh of exhaustion. This was day one of about 1,275 more like it to come. The mountain seemed too big. I needed to spend some time with God in prayer and reading the Bible for strength and encouragement. I could not do this on my own. I needed God to carry me.

After the kids were put to bed that night, I started talking to God. I asked Him to please make Seanny's mediport work so he wouldn't have to have another surgery. I asked Him to please remove whatever was blocking it. Then I left it in God's hands. Next, I asked Him to please help us with our finances. We needed more than we were bringing in, and I was shocked at how much money we needed just that day. Pittsburgh was about forty miles from our house, so that was eighty miles round trip. I drove a beat-up old Suburban that probably got about thirteen miles per gallon. We couldn't afford a newer vehicle, but I didn't know how we were going to pay for just the gas. I didn't want to say much about it to Sean. I know down deep he thought I would be saying he wasn't a good enough provider. I thought he did quite well and was a very hard worker, but unfortunately it wasn't enough. So as I talked to God about this dilemma, I felt His peace surround me. I thanked Him for getting us through the day and was too tired for anything else.

The next time we went to the clinic for Seanny's treatment, his mediport worked! I was so happy that I had to hold back tears. Every miracle, big or small, was such a blessing to me. I was not taking anything for granted.

On the way home, I noticed my gas gauge was nearing empty. Sigh. I would stop at the gas station our friend owned by our house to fill up. After he filled my tank up, I asked how much I owed him. He said, "Nothing."

I started to argue with him that I wasn't allowing him to pay for my gas. He just smiled and said, "Have a good day."

I was so grateful, but part of me felt bad. Pride can be a terrible burden. I didn't want people to know how great our need was, and I definitely didn't want them to think Sean wasn't able to take care of us. I have to admit I was more grateful than embarrassed at the moment. The next time I needed to get gas, the same thing happened. I asked Sean to please talk to them. Sean told them we greatly appreciated what they were doing, but we couldn't keep taking advantage of them.

The owner told Sean, "Listen, I was sworn to secrecy, so don't repeat this. A wealthy man from this area heard about your family's situation. He left his credit card with us and insists on paying for all of Tracey's gas for the next year. He's not the only one who offered. People want to help. Allow them to."

Sean and I were speechless. I don't know if that man had any idea how unbelievably, overwhelmingly grateful we were. What seemed like a small gesture to him was huge to us. Our financial situation was growing worse every day, but this would eliminate one burden. I thanked God so much for putting concern in people's hearts for us. I could see Him working in so many areas of our lives. I also realized that many times when God wants to bless us, He does so through other people.

Seanny had to have a spinal done at his next appointment. They would put a needle into his spine to drain some fluid from it and test it for cancer. He had to lie very still while they did this; if he moved, he could be paralyzed. As we held him down, he started to get nervous. I started singing the "Love Him in the Morning" song. He instantly calmed down and relaxed. The doctor was just amazed at that. His spinal fluid came back clear of cancer. They told me they would do this once a month for the first year. Then they would periodically check it after that. Wow, that meant at least sixteen more to go. The good thing was that Seanny got to pick a toy from the treasure box after any major procedure, such as a spinal or bone marrow test. For a three-year-old, that was exciting news. I swear he took half an hour to pick out a Matchbox car. I didn't mind; he deserved it.

Later that evening, he was so proud to show his sisters the car he earned. They asked what the treasure box was. I explained to them that it was a medium-sized box full of small toys that the children got to pick from after they had any serious test or procedure. The girls thought that was a good idea someone came up with. They wanted to know, if they used their own money, if I would take them to the store so they could buy toys for the kids' treasure box. I never discouraged loving or generous acts, so I told them of course I would. They each had around fifteen dollars, so they took their time finding special toys they thought the kids would like. I was so proud of them. I don't know how their hearts fit into their chests; they were so big.

My parents and Sean's parents insisted that we go out for lunch or something the first weekend I was home. I really didn't want to leave Seanny, but I thought maybe he could use a break from me for an hour or two. Sean's parents came over to watch the kids. We didn't have money to waste, so we decided to go to a drive-through restaurant. After we got our food, we sat in the parking lot eating and talking. Sean had been so tense and wound up from the last three and a half weeks, and I was the one he usually vented to. As we sat there, he told me how hard things had been for him. I know I wasn't overly sympathetic. He was starting to get angry, not at me but at the situation we were in. As I've said, the first emotion he always showed was anger.

We started driving home, and we were both getting frustrated with each other. Sean's response was to drive hard. He was starting to scare me. When we came to a stoplight, I got out of the vehicle. He asked what in the world I was doing. I told him if he wanted to kill himself, that was fine, but my children needed me. I was walking home. He begged me to get back in, and when I started walking, he said he would let me drive. I said fine and got into the driver's seat. We did not say anything to each other. A few miles later, we came to a stop, and Sean got out of the vehicle. I just looked at him and then started driving. I have no idea why he got out. I was driving under the speed limit, and I didn't say anything, so I knew I didn't upset him.

When I got home, Sean's parents asked me where he was. I said he would be coming soon. I didn't know what to tell them. Sean and I kept a lot about ourselves private. They said they needed to be somewhere, so they had to go. I thanked them for coming and said we'd see them soon. Now I was nervous. I knew when Sean got home from his five-mile walk, World War III would break out. I tried not to think about it as the minutes on the clock ticked by. When he finally got home, he looked at me and said, "Why didn't you pick me up?"

I said to him, "Why did you get out? I figured you just needed some air."

His response was, "You don't play right. I picked you up; you were supposed to pick me up."

And for some reason, I started to laugh. Then Sean joined in laughing. God diffused the tense situation and actually allowed us to see the humor in it. Our lives were so overwhelmingly difficult at that time that we didn't always know how to handle it. I know now that love was the only thing that got us through it.

Chapter 6

The days started going by in a similar fashion. Three days a week, I took Seanny to the clinic. Seanny had to take between ten and forty pills a day at home, depending on what day it was. There was one he took every day to help prevent him from getting pneumonia. I never understood why, but for some reason it was extremely dangerous for someone with leukemia to get pneumonia or chickenpox. He was becoming a pro at swallowing pills. I was becoming a neat freak. I was told to keep germs away from Seanny, so I went to war with dirt and filth. I probably washed my hands on average at least fifteen times a day.

Then I had another particularly hard day. One morning I let Seanny sleep in because he didn't have an appointment in Pittsburgh. When I went into his room to check on him, he was just sitting up. When I looked at his pillow, there was hair all over it. I ran my hands over his head, and there was hair covering my hands. Oh, no, my baby was losing his hair! I knew this was coming, but actually seeing it was a different matter. I had to quickly choose how to respond.

I sucked in a deep breath, smiled at Seanny, and said, "Looks like your hair is coming out. You're going to be so cute as a baldy. You will be my bald eagle."

He smiled back at me and said, "Cool!"

I sat on the bed next to him and gently combed his hair until there was nothing left. It came off so easily. I knew if I didn't do this, it would just make him itch until it was all gone. Even though this was just temporary, my heart hurt nonetheless. I hugged him and told him he was the handsomest boy I had ever seen. He hugged me and told me I was his pretty momma. It's hard to stay feeling sad when you're so blessed.

Anyone who saw Seanny could tell he was on chemo. He was bald, pale, and had such chubby cheeks from his steroids. And yet some people were oblivious. I remember being at a gas station one time, pumping gas with Seanny standing right beside me. On the other side of the pump was a wealthy-looking middle-aged man.

He said to me, right in front of my son, "That's a stupid haircut for a kid, especially this time of the year."

Anger swept over me like a tidal wave. My first instinct was to tackle him.

Somehow, I calmly replied while staring him in the eyes, "That's what chemo will do to you."

The man looked shocked and sick at the same time. He quickly got in his car and left. It didn't faze Seanny in the least. I just winked at him, and he gave me one of his incredible smiles back. I had the best kids in the whole world.

Alysha Rae made a lot of the trips to the clinic with Seanny and me. She was only four and a half years old and not yet in school. On the days I knew Seanny was getting a transfusion, I would pack coloring books and crayons, books, and playing cards in a backpack for her. Those were five- to eight-hour days just at the clinic. She never complained about coming along; I actually think she enjoyed herself. She was a low-maintenance kid and could entertain herself easily. She would ask me what they were doing to Seanny at different times. Even though she was busy coloring or looking at books, she always kept her eye on him. Brittini and Alysha were very protective of their baby brother.

I had read in the Bible in James 5:14 and 15: "Is anyone among you sick? Let them call the elders of the church to pray over them and anoint them with oil in the name of the Lord. And the prayer said in faith will make the sick person well; the Lord will raise him up."

I wanted to be obedient to God, so we called the elders of our church to come and pray over Seanny. They very willingly came to our house to pray. The prayers went something like this: "Dear God, if it's Your will, please heal this child. If it's not Your will, fill them with Your peace. Give them strength to endure whatever You decide."

Although I was so appreciative of their willingness to come, I was not so happy with their prayer. I thanked the Lord for them, but I also thanked the Lord for showing me what His will is. I could boldly pray over my son, knowing God heard and was answering my prayers.

A few weeks after we came home from the hospital, the local police decided to have a golf outing to benefit Seanny. I still had a hard time believing so many people wanted to help us. Sean asked me to bring Seanny down at the end of the tournament so people could meet him. His blood counts were decent, so I took him to the golf course. All the people treated us like royalty. When they gathered around to announce the winners, Seanny and I sat at the table toward the back to listen. The first-place winners received a large check as their prize. The leader of the group took the check, walked back, and handed it to me. I whispered a soft thank you, blinking quickly to hold back tears. The second- and third-place winners did the same thing. I could feel tears slipping down my cheeks. Did these people know how their acts of kindness were affecting us? Yes, we really needed the money, but their love and support were just as necessary. The money raised that day was astounding. All I can say about it is wow!

I always wanted to do something fun or special with the kids after Seanny had a big test and chemo. If his blood counts were good enough for him to be allowed in public, I would occasionally take them to Chuck E. Cheese. It was about half an hour away from our home. The kids would get so excited just anticipating it. I remember one particular time as we were driving home, and the kids were eating the cotton candy they had won, we could see a bunch of protestors along the main street of town. The kids asked me what was going on, and I said I wasn't sure yet. As we got closer, I could see the signs they were holding. They were protesting abortion, and their signs showed graphic pictures of babies after the procedure. My heart skipped a beat, and I felt incredibly sick to my stomach. I told the kids not to look at the pictures because they were for adults only to see. Who was I kidding? No one should see those pictures.

As I drove by those people, I felt their condemning eyes looking directly at me. I was so ashamed and embarrassed. I was hurt and angry at the same time. It threw the past in my face so hard and quickly. But I was angry because they didn't know how their signs affected people. How would they like people holding signs up of their mistakes and sins for them to see? I agree with them that abortion is wrong, but I disagree with their approach. One of the biggest mistakes a person can make is to judge another person's sins. Jesus even said, "Let he who has never sinned throw the first stone." Every sin, whether it is gossiping, lusting, lying, or abortion, takes us away from God. I can't believe some people feel more righteous than others because they feel they aren't as big of a sinner as someone else. Christians could do a lot more damage to Satan's kingdom by showing love instead of judgment. Besides, I didn't need them to make me feel guilty. I carried that burden with me every day.

In October of that year, another one of our friends who owned a store had a huge Oktoberfest to benefit Seanny. I didn't even know about it until a couple of days before it happened. Radio stations were announcing the event, and it was in the newspapers, but somehow I was oblivious to it. So many people came. The amount of money raised was beyond incredible. I didn't even know how to begin to thank people for all they had done.

Although all this money helped immensely, there was still a huge financial burden for Sean and me. When Seanny got sick, I quit my part-time job immediately. Even with me working, we were short meeting our monthly budget. We had great insurance, but paying even 10 percent of the medical bills was huge. Seanny was on so many medications that I was getting to know the pharmacists by name. The expenses just kept going up and up. I tried to put the weight of this problem into God's hand, but every time we came up short or got an unexpected bill that was enormous, I would take the problem back and start to worry. Financial issues can be so hard on a marriage. We kept plugging along, though. Sean was still taking on any side job he could find. Although it was such a blessing, he didn't know how to slow down. What started as God providing some extra work for Sean turned into an obsession. Sean wouldn't tell anyone no. Sometimes he would work twenty hours a day. Some days he would work on the side for eight hours and get paid the total of twenty dollars.

The lack of sleep made him extra grumpy when he was around me or the kids. I felt like a single mother most of the time. I know each man deals with stress differently, just like women. Sean's way of coping was to stay busy and work. We really did need the money, but this was insane. If I complained to Sean that he didn't spend any time with us, he would say he would slow down but to be prepared to lose the house or something. What a predicament.

Our family doctor and his wife recommended Seanny to the local Make-A-Wish foundation. The foundation contacted us to see if they could grant a wish for Seanny. I told them that was a wonderful idea. They came to our house the next week to talk to Seanny and our family. They explained that they granted wishes to children who have life-threatening illnesses. They asked Seanny if there was anything special he would like. Immediately he responded, "A Pontiac GTO Judge."

I know they had to think we put him up to this. What three-year-old asks for an old muscle car? They told him they were not able to give cars as gifts. He wasn't able to go on a vacation because his counts kept fluctuating and going way too low. They asked him if he would like a computer. They explained that he could play car games and design cars on one. He thought that sounded like a good idea. They said they would see what they could arrange and get back to us soon.

In November, a limo came to pick up our family at home to take us all on Seanny's Make-A-Wish day. We were all so excited. We had never ridden in a limo before. They took us to a grand opening of a Best Buy store. Seanny was named the honorary manager and got to cut the ribbon to open the store. They presented him with a computer, printer, games, and a desk. They let Brittini and Alysha each choose any movie from the store they wanted. I thought it was so thoughtful that they included the girls. After being treated like royalty for the day, we were on the way home and went through the drive-through at McDonald's in the limo. It was a day none of us will ever forget.

Any time Seanny got a fever, we had to take him to the local emergency room. We were never allowed to give a fever reducer, such as Tylenol, until they drew blood so they could test it. One time his fever was high and out of control. By the time we made it to the hospital, it had reached 105 degrees. The hospital said he needed to get to Children's Hospital immediately. They ordered an ambulance to take us there. As they were loading Seanny, he said he couldn't ride in the ambulance. I thought he might be scared, so I reassured him that I was going with him. He said that wasn't the problem. This ambulance was a Ford, and he could only ride in Chevys. Sigh. Only my son. I told him we'd make an exception this time, and we wouldn't tell anyone he rode in a Ford.

It turned out he just had a virus. His immune system was just too weak to fight it off. They admitted him for three days and gave him antibiotics. Seanny's immune system was so compromised that a cold or virus could put him in the hospital. We tried hard to keep him away from anyone who was sick, but with Brittini being in school, she brought a lot of germs home. Plus we were going to the clinic on a regular basis. We were around a lot of people there, too. It was impossible to keep him in a bubble.

There were always too many kids getting treatment at the clinic when we went. Stupid cancer…it infuriated me. There were four kids we saw almost every time we were there. We got to know each one of them and their families well. One little girl got to go to Disney World for her Make-A-Wish day. A few weeks later, there was a huge picture hanging up in the playroom at the clinic of Dorothy from *The Wizard of Oz*. The caption read, "There's no place like home." I asked one of the nurses about that picture. She said the family of the little girl bought it in memory of her. I was in shock. We had just seen her. It was a harsh reminder of how fragile life is for these children. Satan had a field day trying to scare me and consume me with sadness. I had to immediately take my thoughts captive, like the Bible tells us to, and decide what I would do.

The Bible tells a story of how Jesus came walking on the water to His disciples during the night in the middle of a storm. Peter cried out, "Lord, if it is you, tell me to come out and join you."

Jesus said, "Come."

Peter got out of the boat and started walking on water. As the storm raged, Peter took his eyes off of Jesus and looked at the storm and crashing waves.

He started to sink. Jesus reached out and saved him and said, "Peter, why did you doubt?"

I realized that I needed to focus on Jesus instead of all that was going on around me. With Jesus, nothing is impossible.

Chapter 7

It was getting close to Christmas. That year, the holiday took on a whole new meaning. I was so glad we were all together. The weekend before Christmas, we heard fire sirens in front of our house. We looked outside, and there sat the local fire engine. Then we saw someone getting out of the vehicle. It was Santa! The kids were so excited. Sean and I were shocked. Somehow they found out that Seanny's counts were low, so he couldn't go to the mall to see Santa. So Santa came to him. I was struggling to keep my composure; the gratitude I felt toward these people was enormous. Santa, of course, had a big bag of toys for my children. After spending about an hour at our home, Santa said the fire engine had to get back to work, and he had to go with them because that's where his reindeer were waiting for him. Smile.

We've always spent Christmas Eve going from Sean's parents' to my parents' and then to church. This year was different. Sean, Brittini, Alysha Rae, Seanny, and me got up very early in the morning and went together to Seanny's chemo appointment at the clinic. We arrived early, so we went across the street to the hospital cafeteria to have breakfast together. Seanny liked that the whole family was there. After his appointment was done, we stopped at both sets of parents' for a short visit. Seanny usually felt nauseous after chemotherapy, and his counts were a little low, so we didn't stay long at either home. Even though we didn't get to do all of our normal traditions, this year was the best Christmas we ever had. As I read my children the Christmas story, my heart was especially touched at how God the Father sent His only Son, Jesus, with the sole purpose of dying for us. I had a deeper appreciation of how hard that must have been for God.

Christmas came and went so fast. Seanny was still going for treatment three days a week. Now that he had been receiving treatments for over four months, it was really taking a toll on his body. He got tired very easily, and his stomach was upset frequently. You could tell when he needed another transfusion. He would get so pale and incredibly tired. Considering everything, he was still a normal little boy. He loved to build with his Lincoln Logs, play with Matchbox cars, and use his computer. When he felt up to it, we played ball. I think his favorite thing to do was to agitate his sisters. We didn't go out among the general public very much. Even church was frowned upon by his doctors. Every Friday night, I would have a movie night/sleepover with the kids on our living room floor. We would get our sleeping bags out, pop popcorn, play games, and watch a movie. They loved this, and I looked forward to it as much as they did. I refused to allow any of us to sit around feeling sorry for ourselves.

I always told my children, "If you look at all the blessings God has given you, you won't have time to look at the things that you aren't happy about."

Seanny got another fever, so we had to take him to the local ER again. It was the middle of the night, so it was fairly busy. They always took him back to a room right away so he wouldn't have to be around anyone who was sick. After they drew some blood to have tested, we were sitting there waiting for the results. That could take hours. We could hear an older lady moaning and screaming a few rooms down from us. It was a bit disturbing. Seanny grabbed my hand and said we needed to pray for her right away because she was having a "bow and arrow" test. That was how he said "bone marrow test." I smiled to myself. I was thinking how funny it was that he related people being in pain to having bone marrow tests. Nonetheless, we knelt down on that hospital floor and prayed for her. When we were through, we got up and saw a nurse. We didn't realize she was there.

She asked, "How in the world did you know that lady was having a bone marrow test?"

I looked at her surprised and speechless.

Then she asked, "Did you notice she settled down while you were praying? She's been calm ever since."

I looked at my son and smiled. God was working through Seanny for His glory. It was just the beginning.

During Seanny's three-day hospital stay, Alysha had her testing for kindergarten registration. I unfortunately missed this, too. I found out she scored very well. I hated not being there for every special event in my children's lives. I really didn't miss that many, but one was too many for me. They were moments I could never get back. I didn't regret being with Seanny, though. I just wished I could be in two places at once.

I remember my first Mother's Day after Seanny was diagnosed with leukemia. Seanny couldn't sit up to get out of bed. He was so weak and tired. I carried him to the living room couch and laid him on it. Then I called his doctor and told him how Seanny was acting. He said it wasn't unusual for a child who was taking the amount of chemo that Seanny was to act that way. He said Seanny should have been, and will continue to be, like this for a while. If it gets worse, they can give him a shot that would help some. Well, I didn't like it. It broke my heart to see him just lying there, too weak to even feed himself. By evening, Seanny was no better. Brittini and Alysha asked me to lay him on the living room floor. I asked them why. They said he was being attacked, so we needed to march around him seven times, singing and praising God… just like Joshua did at the Battle of Jericho. I agreed. So there we were, singing and dancing around Seanny as he lay there.

The next morning when Seanny woke up, he jumped out of bed and came running to see me. He said he felt all better and wanted to play. I stood there staring at him, amazed at the difference in my boy. I was starting to understand why God said we need to have faith like children. My girls saw what God did in the Bible for His people, and they knew He would do the same for us. Period. We might have looked crazy to people, but I know we pulled down strongholds that evening when we marched around Seanny praising God. It was miraculous.

I was reading my Bible one evening, and I came across Hebrews 4:12: "The word of God is living and active. Sharper than any double-edged sword, it penetrates even to dividing soul and spirit, joints and marrow…" Did that really just say "marrow"? I remember the doctor telling me the marrow is the deepest part of your *physical* body. God is concerned about our bodies, and His word gets to the deepest part of it. His word is life, healing, and peace. John, chapter one, says, "In the beginning was the word, and the word was with God, and the word was God." Wow… God's word is Jesus! And the word goes through the joints and into the marrow. I believed Seanny was healed from the first week in the hospital. It was done in the spirit realm; the physical just hadn't manifested yet. After reading this, I knew God was reaffirming this was true.

I put Post-It notes with scriptures on them all over our house. I wanted to keep God's word, His promises, in view at all times. I would read the scriptures and put our family members' names in them. For instance, according to Isaiah 53:5, "And by Jesus's stripes, Seanny is healed." Isaiah 54:17 says, "No weapon formed against Sean, Brittini, Alysha, Seanny, or Tracey shall prosper." I had over twenty different scriptures posted around our house, and I would quote them out loud multiple times a day.

One of my favorite verses is Romans 4:17, "God gives life to the dead and calls those things that are not as though they were." God revealed to me again that words are powerful. God used words to call the universe into existence. God used words and spoke about things to come thousands of years before they happened, such as the birth of His Son. He was teaching me to line up my words with His word, and facts would change. You see, facts can change, but the truth can't. The fact was Seanny did have cancer. The truth was Jesus healed him. Faith believes before it sees. I was through doubting.

Every time Seanny was through with a chemo appointment, he would say, "Come on, Mom. Let's go get your 'burban and then go get something to eat."

One day a nurse asked if she could talk to me for a moment. She asked me how I was really handling everything. I told her I had so much hope and that I knew everything was going to be fine. She proceeded to ask me why I have to drink bourbon every time we leave the clinic. I was dumbfounded. What was she talking about?

She said, "Seanny always says, 'Let's go get your bourbon.'"

Oh, my goodness! I started to laugh so hard I cried. I explained to her that I drive a Chevy Suburban, and Seanny has always called it "Mommy's 'burban." The nurse was so embarrassed; she said that there were a few of them that thought I might have a drinking problem. I'm so glad God gave me a good sense of humor. Smile.

In May 1998, seven and a half months into Seanny's treatments, the American Cancer Society called us. They were having their second annual Relay for Life in our county. They wanted to know if Seanny would cut the ribbon to start the twenty-four-hour event. They also asked if he could lead the first lap designated for people fighting cancer and for cancer survivors. I said we'd be honored to participate. When we arrived at the stadium for this event, I was shocked at how many people were there. It was a beautiful, warm, sunny day. So much was going on. There were booths set up everywhere. Some were selling food, others had crafts, and a few even had games set up. Music was blaring over the speakers. It was very festive. There were a few speakers before the relay even got started. Andy Russell, a former Pittsburgh Steeler, was one of them. They called Seanny, Sean, and me out of the bleachers to come down so Seanny could cut the ribbon. After we got on the track, they called for all the survivors to come and join him as he led the survivors' lap. I was stunned at how many people were making their way to the track. Some were missing limbs, some were bald like Seanny, some were in wheelchairs, some were on stretchers, and others looked like the picture of health. Seanny was the only child on the track, thank God.

As they introduced Seanny and told everyone that he was currently fighting leukemia, people started cheering and clapping. When he cut the ribbon, the survivors started making their way around the track. It was an emotional moment for me to see so many people fighting and affected by this awful disease. When we made it to the finish line, people were just going crazy. They were cheering and shouting their encouragement. We got to meet and talk to so many wonderful people. We shared God's love with everyone we met. It was such an inspiring day.

Chapter 8

A year into Seanny's chemo, he had to have another bone marrow test and spinal. We arrived early to the clinic that day. After the tests, he would have his chemo treatment. As always, I was right next to Seanny, singing. He was given a drug to twilight him for the bone marrow test. This always made him act as though he was drunk. After the tests were done, we were sitting in the playroom with Seanny as his chemo dripped through his IV. They called us back into an exam room. The doctor told us that his spinal test came back leukemia-free, and so did his bone marrow test. Seanny was in remission. What? Was she agreeing with me that Seanny was healed?

As she saw the look on my face, she quickly explained, "Seanny is now in remission. That means as of right now, there is no leukemia in him. That does not mean he's cured, though. He still has about two and a half years of chemo left, and his immune system is still very much compromised. The leukemia could come back at any time. I don't want to downplay the good news, but I want to be realistic. Another piece of good news is Seanny only has to come in for treatments once every four weeks now."

I could feel the tears blurring my vision. As I looked at my son, I was looking at a child who had no cancer in his body. I knew it was never coming back. I started to thank Jesus right then and there. He was officially in remission. We were going to celebrate. We threw a party at the police lodge. Around one hundred people came to help us celebrate. We got to testify to God's goodness and healing. I knew we still had a long road ahead of us, but for now we wanted to praise God for what He had done and what He was doing.

Halfway through the party, we could hear a police siren. We all went out onto the deck to see what was going on. Up the long gravel driveway came the General Lee being chased by a police car. Now, for those of you who don't understand this, the General Lee was the car on the *Dukes of Hazzard* TV show that Bo and Luke Duke drove. My family loved to watch this program, and we had almost every tape of the show that was available. What a nice surprise. Seanny was so excited. They asked if he could go for a ride in the car, and he climbed through the window just like the Dukes did! We didn't tell him the door could open. We couldn't have asked for a more beautiful day or a better reason to celebrate.

Alysha started kindergarten that fall of 1998. It was strange to have just Seanny with me at home. We were already so close; now we had even more one-on-one time. I remember an afternoon when my sister called and asked if she could take Seanny and me bowling. I thought that sounded like fun, and there wouldn't be many people there that early in the afternoon. When we arrived, we only saw one group of teenagers in the whole place. Good, not too many people there to spread germs. As we were bowling, we could hear the teenagers laughing. I could see anger in my sister's eyes. I asked her what was wrong, and she said the teenagers were making fun of Seanny being bald.

She looked at me and said, "We could take them."

My sister was only twenty years old, so I knew I had to be the mature one.

I looked at her and said, "Of course we could, either in a fight or at bowling, but they're not worth it."

We did glare over in their direction, making sure we made eye contact, and gave them the evil eye. It was a silent challenge. Oh my.

Around Sean's thirtieth birthday, he was working at putting on a roof for someone. While he was on the slanted roof, he was squatted down to nail some shingles on. He pivoted while squatting to pick up some nails behind him, and he felt his knee explode. He couldn't move his leg and was in excruciating pain. He had to call for help because he couldn't use his leg to get down the ladder. A fire truck had to come on the scene and use their bucket to get him off the roof. I got a call saying Sean got hurt while on a roof and that he was on his way to the ER. Those were all the details I was told. I had no idea how serious the situation was. So I got in Sean's car, because it was the fastest one we owned, and made remarkable time to the emergency room. Sean was just being released when I got there. He came out using crutches. At least he was conscious. Sean had torn his meniscus, and surgery was required to fix it.

My husband was beyond frustrated with the situation. He was worried about not being able to make any extra money and how much his medical expenses would be. I was concerned down deep, too, but I told him it would be a good time for him to rest and take it easy. I knew God didn't want Sean to get hurt, but I believe God can turn any situation around and use it for good. Sean got through the surgery well. The first few days he had so much pain he could hardly stand it. I should have sung to him, but I don't think he would have appreciated it. Thankfully, after those initial days, his recovery progressed right according to schedule. I have to admit we tormented Sean occasionally. When he was in the recliner one day, the kids and I started squirting him with our squirt guns. We knew he couldn't get up to chase us or to retaliate, so we took advantage of the situation. Seanny kept teasing his dad that it looked like he peed himself. We drenched him! He was a pretty good sport with us. I think we caused him to recuperate much quicker than he thought possible. Smile.

Since Seanny's counts were doing better, we decided it was time to start going to church again. We didn't realize there had been a split in the church, and only a handful of people were still attending. What had happened? Actually, I didn't want to know. I loved all the people there and didn't want to hear anything bad or negative about any of them. I decided to find another home church. I asked God to help me find one that loved to praise and worship Him, believed in healing, loved each other, believed in the baptism of the Holy Spirit, had good children's programs, and had a strong youth group. I didn't even know if a church like that existed. I prayed for God to lead us to just the right one. I found a church for us on the first try. Well, God led us, and we obediently followed.

Chapter 9

Sean was having trouble at work. It all stemmed from the arrests he had made on the family back before Seanny got sick. He was being falsely accused and threatened. We didn't realize just how serious the problems were about to get from this.

One night Seanny woke up with a fever. I bundled him up and rushed him to the emergency room like I always did when he had a fever. When I was checking him in, I was told our health insurance was no longer valid. What?! My husband was still working the same job he had for the past eight years, and nothing had changed. They told me they would treat Seanny but to get it straightened out as soon as possible. I was very frustrated but was too focused on Seanny to give it a second thought.

I talked to Sean about it the next day, and he said when he went to work later that day he would check into it. He found out that because of what he was being falsely accused of, some people who didn't like him were planning on firing him. They had already canceled his insurance. They had no grounds or legal right to do this. He was still working, and no one even informed us of this. They told us it was a mistake, and they would fix the problem immediately.

A few months later, Sean was suspended without pay from his job until further notice. They denied him unemployment, and because he was still a policeman, he wasn't allowed to have another full-time job. I couldn't believe what was happening. We had no source of income. We had no idea how long this would go on or if he would even have a job to go back to. Sean was beyond angry and frustrated with the injustice of the situation. I knew the only person who could help us was God.

I got alone with God and asked Him what we should do. I told Him that He had beyond earned my trust, and I would follow His lead. He had taught me how to live by faith for healing. Now He was about to do the same with our finances.

He showed me what He thought about this situation in Proverbs 17:15, "Acquitting the guilty and condemning the innocent—the Lord detests them both."

I knew the outcome was in the Lord's hands. I asked Him to show me what to do in the meantime. He told me again to guard the words that came out of my mouth. He told me to find verses that pertained to our situation and claim them over Sean. One of my favorites was Isaiah 54:17, "No weapon formed against you will prosper, and you will refute every tongue that accuses you. 'This is the heritage of the servants of the Lord, and this is their vindication from me,' declares the Lord."

God also showed me the importance of tithing… giving Him 10 percent of our money. He said He multiplies what you give Him, but He needs something to work with. I thought, *Okay, Lord, I will be obedient. We don't have an income right now, but whatever we get, I'll tithe.*

God was teaching me that He is our source, not man or any job. God expects man to work. It says in His word that if you don't work, you don't eat. But we are not to rely on anyone or anything other than God. I was getting a crash course on this.

After a couple of weeks, nothing changed. It would have been so easy to give in to worry, fear, and hate. I wasn't giving up or giving in. I had made a decision, and we were trusting God. I knew He was working the situation behind the scenes, where we couldn't see. That's what faith is according to Hebrews 11:1: "Now faith is being sure of what we hope for and certain of what we do not see."

If Sean detailed a car for fifty dollars, I would immediately put five dollars away for church. If I babysat for thirty dollars a day, I'd immediately take three dollars and put back our tithe. Down deep the voice of lies was telling me that wasn't even a fraction of what we needed. I was determined to listen to God, the Voice of Truth.

The lies and gossip that were going on behind our backs were hurtful. It would have been easy to get bitter with people. God instructed me to forgive and let Him handle it. I was fine with that because I couldn't deal with it.

After about three weeks without a steady income, the unemployment office called and said Sean qualified to receive it. We asked how that happened; we were turned down. They said they investigated the case and found no cause for denial. Wow, we were so excited. Even though unemployment was only about 50 percent of what Sean had been making, it was something.

I remember a few months into this whole ordeal, I had thirty-five dollars in my purse. That was all we had for groceries for the five of us for two weeks or more. I was on my way to church, and I was thinking about how to make the most of our money to get by. Praise and worship started, and I pushed those thoughts aside and started enjoying spending time with Jesus. It was time for the offering plate to be passed around, so we all took our seats. I heard God tell me in my spirit, "Put your thirty-five dollars in the offering."

I thought, *Oh, Lord, did I hear You right? It's all I have.*

I heard Him say again, "Put your thirty-five dollars in the offering."

Okay, Lord, I thought and smiled. *This thirty-five dollars wasn't even going to last a week. If you want us to fast, so be it.*

When the plate was in front of me, I dropped in everything I had. We had no grocery money even after the unemployment check. I felt God's peace surround me. I loved the Lord, and I trusted whatever He had planned.

On the way home, the kids asked if we were going to the grocery store. I told them not right then. How was I going to tell Sean that I had given all of our money away? When we got home, I opened our front screen door, and there was an envelope. *That's strange*, I thought. *I wonder who put that there.*

I opened the envelope and caught my breath. There was $350 in it. There was no note or explanation. I instantly raised my hands in praise and gratitude to God. I sure could buy a lot more groceries with $350 than thirty-five dollars. God had everything under control. I just needed to trust Him.

Finally, after months of this situation dragging on, Sean had a hearing to settle everything. I went to the building where his hearing was to take place the next day, and I drove around it seven times. I prayed over the building and claimed God's Shalom peace over it. I drew a faith line around the place, declaring that no lying or evil spirits would have any influence. I was getting prepared. We were about to go to battle.

The next day, Sean went up against a lot of big and influential people. There sure were a lot more of them than there were of us. I overheard someone say, "This is a David and Goliath battle."

Did they realize who won that battle? Peace encompassed me. God was using our enemies to confirm our victory.

I sat beside Sean with my Bible open in plain view. I prayed silently the whole time. After hours of testimonies, the arbitrator told us he would let us know his decision. We were told that could take many weeks, even months. Well, less than a week later, we got a call that Sean won his case. They found him not guilty on all counts. The arbitrator said he made his decision quickly because it was so easy. He thought the charges and the way they were handled were ridiculous. So after eight months of being suspended from his job, Sean went back to work. He was fully reimbursed for his time off. There was no explanation of how we made it through those months. God had worked another miracle in our lives.

Chapter 10

After the first year that Seanny had cut the ribbon for the American Cancer Society's Relay for Life, we entered our own team in it. Our team name was Sean's Super Sports. For the noncar people out there, some Chevy muscle cars with special packages were called SS. The SS stood for Super Sport. Hence our team name. Each member of our team proudly wore their Sean's Super Sport t-shirts with the Bible verse Philippians 4:13 on the back: "I can do all things through Christ, who gives me strength." Seanny again cut the ribbon to open the relay. So many wonderful, caring people were a part of our team. Some would walk an hour; others would walk six. We always had someone representing our team on the track during the twenty-four hours the relay was held. We all had such a fun time and got to meet so many courageous people. One year Seanny won "prince of the relay." Another year, when Alysha Rae was thirteen years old, she entered the hot dog-eating contest and won. She even competed against men. In Alysha's defense, she was never that big of an eater. Our family was just highly competitive, so she practically swallowed them whole… at least that's what it looked like when they came back up!

Sean and I decided to hold Seanny back a year before he started kindergarten. He still had a little over one year left of chemo, so we figured why chance him being around so many kids and germs. Seanny was still going to the clinic every four weeks for a checkup and chemotherapy and was still taking between five and twenty-six pills at home every day as part of his treatment. He was doing well, although he had to stay in the hospital a couple of times that year because he spiked a fever. Each time they had to run blood work on him, and each time it came back fine.

In the fall of 2000, Seanny got to start kindergarten. The first day of school was hard for me, and I had to tell myself not to get in my vehicle and follow the bus. Not only did he fight to get to this day, but he was also my baby. I told myself at least he wasn't alone. Brittini was in fourth grade, and Alysha was in second grade, and they all rode the same bus and went to the same school. They would look out for each other. We had a habit of always reading devotions together in the morning and praying. Then we would read the ninety-first Psalm over our family; it was such a powerful word of protection. I knew my children were in God's hands, surrounded by angels. I just had a protective streak a mile long.

Seanny liked school a lot. As much as he loved his mom, I think he enjoyed hanging around other people besides me. Holding him back a year was a good idea for many reasons. He was more mature and advanced because of it. The other kids treated him just like they treated everyone else. Seanny was still going through chemo but only had a couple of months left. About five weeks into the school year, chickenpox broke out. The school nurse called me right away to come pick Seanny up from school. I took him to his doctor to be checked out. He had no sign of chickenpox, but the doctor told us to pull him out of school until the virus was through and then wait another month before sending him back. It looked like he wouldn't be going back until the next spring. Seanny was okay with that. The kids in his class made him cards and mailed them to him. A tutor came out about once a week to bring him his lessons. I enjoyed having him home with me again.

One morning, Seanny woke up with red bumps all over his back and stomach. Oh, no, he had chickenpox. I could feel fear encompassing me. They told me if he got it, it could be fatal.

I immediately knelt down beside Seanny and prayed, "Thank You, Jesus, for loving Seanny and healing him. Thank You for protecting him and taking chickenpox away from him. We trust You and thank You for taking care of us."

Then I spoke to the problem like Jesus commands us to.

I said out loud, "Chickenpox, we rebuke you from hurting Seanny. We command you to leave him and not harm him in any way. He is God's property, and he is healed by the stripes of Jesus."

In the Bible, Jesus says He had been given all authority. Then He gave it to us. We are to imitate Jesus and do as He did. He commanded us to.

As quickly as the fear came, it left. I called the doctor, and he said if Seanny got a temperature over a hundred degrees to bring him to Children's Hospital immediately. He never did. He barely even itched. He was all cleared up within a week and a half.

The next month, on October 20, 2000, Seanny had another bone marrow test, and a spinal and chemotherapy appointment. After the tests, we were waiting in the playroom for the doctor to call us back with the results. Finally, we were taken back to the exam room. The doctor told us that all of Seanny's tests came back cancer-free, and this would be his last chemotherapy treatment. I knelt down right then and there and thanked Jesus from the bottom of my heart for all He had done. Then I cried. I felt like my heart was exploding with gratitude and joy! After more than three years of treatment, we were done. The mountain had been made flat. Seanny was alive and had beaten the odds.

The doctor was happy along with us but wanted to let us know that Seanny wasn't considered cured until he hit the ten-year mark. He would have to come in once a month for the next three months for a checkup and have his mediport flushed, then twice a year for a year, then once a year. After three months of good checkups, they would surgically take his mediport out. He said for the next year, Seanny's immune system would be compromised, and we would still need to be careful with him being around a lot of people, especially if they were sick. Nothing the doctor said could dampen my happiness.

I love how God works out the timing of everything. Everyone told me that turning thirty is hard. I didn't think it would be, but because of all the negative words, I wasn't looking forward to it. The day after Seanny's last chemotherapy appointment was my thirtieth birthday. I had never been happier, and I remember my thirtieth birthday as being one of the best days of my life! Smile.

That Sunday, when the church service was over and people were leaving, I went down to the altar by myself. I just wanted to thank God for all He had done for us. I had come to God so many times, mostly asking Him for things. Now I just wanted to thank Him. As I was talking to Him, I could feel myself starting to cry. I rarely did this in public, but I couldn't help it. My heart was so full, I couldn't stop the tears. The pastor saw me, came up, and asked if I needed prayer for anything. I said no; I just needed time to thank God. He smiled and left me alone. God had not only kept all of His promises, but He blessed us abundantly in every way. I didn't want to take any of it for granted. God had proven He was more than enough in every situation we encountered. And I thanked Him.

It was Christmastime again, and Seanny still wasn't allowed to go back to school because of the chickenpox. The school always had a Santa's secret workshop, where the kids could bring in money to buy Christmas presents for their families. My girls loved to do this each year. We got a call from the school asking if we could bring Seanny there that evening if there were no other children in the school building. We said of course we would. We had no idea what was going on. They had left the Santa's secret workshop up so that Seanny could go shopping like all the other kids. They even had Santa there to help him. We stayed in the hall as he shopped. When he was finally done, he had bags of gifts for his family. Sean asked how much he owed for everything, and they said nothing. Sean insisted on paying, but they refused. We had learned to accept people's generosity and just tried to express how much their kindness and love meant to us.

In January 2001, Seanny was scheduled for outpatient surgery to get his mediport taken out. Although I still liked to be right by his side, I wasn't fearful of him going into surgery without me like the first time. God had brought me so far, and I knew He'd be right there with Seanny. As Sean and I sat in the waiting room, I wrote our family doctor a letter. I thanked him for allowing God to lead him in sending Seanny so quickly to Children's Hospital when he suspected that Seanny had leukemia. I thanked him for always being there for us throughout the past few years and for helping to instruct us. I told him God had guided him to help us in so many ways. A few months later, his wife told me he received that letter on his fiftieth birthday. She said it touched his heart and that he kept it in his office.

As I sat there reflecting on the last few years, I realized that Seanny never once complained or said he wasn't going to the doctor's office or to get his chemo. He didn't look forward to it, but when I told him it was time to go, he never gave me a hard time. That in itself was a huge miracle.

When they called us back to the recovery room, Seanny was just coming out of the anesthesia. He had blood all over his mouth and cheeks. It looked like he had been in a boxing match. What had happened? The nurse quickly explained that Seanny had a loose tooth, so they had to pull it out before surgery. It was a relief to know that was all it was.

As Seanny was starting to come to and make sense, he asked the nurse if he could keep his mediport. She smiled and told him sure.

After a few hours, we got to take Seanny home. He, of course, wanted to eat. We got him and the family hot wings to celebrate. Throughout the day, Seanny received numerous bouquets of balloons and gifts. It was a day to remember.

Seanny was finally allowed to go back to kindergarten and finish the last couple of months of school. We decided we were going to throw a huge chemo-over/mediport-out party. Sean and I wanted it to be a party for all three of our kids. Not only had Seanny been through a lot and come out victorious, but so did our girls. They never complained about Seanny getting more of my time than they did, and they never acted jealous. They prayed for Seanny almost as much as I did. They helped in any way they could. This was a family victory and celebration.

Over two hundred people showed up for our party. We decorated the hall in a car theme. Each table had a ceramic flowerpot full of balloons. The flowerpots had Matthew 19:26 painted on them: "With God all things are possible." We had so much food and so many desserts. Someone even hired a DJ to come and play music so there could be dancing. Halfway through the party, I got up to give our testimony. As I stood in front of all those people, I was nervous. I took a deep breath and started to tell our story—not all of it, but what God had done for Seanny. As I looked around, people were crying.

God was using our story to touch people's hearts. I remember how God told me that first night in the hospital so long ago that He was going to touch thousands of people with our testimony. It was coming to pass, and I was just in awe.

About a year after this, Seanny had a checkup at the clinic. They drew some blood and then sent us to an exam room. The doctor came in and gave Seanny a physical. He said he looked healthy and that he was going to go look at his blood and be back in. The laboratory was right across the hall from our room. I could see the doctor checking out Seanny's blood under a microscope. He kept looking and looking at it. It was taking way too long. I could feel fear coming on me like a tidal wave. God instantly started talking to my spirit. He said I had a choice to make quickly. I could either give in to fear, or I could take authority over the situation. Quietly I started talking. I rebuked the fear and told Satan that Seanny was healed. I told his blood counts to line up with the word of God and be perfect. The doctor came back in the room, and I was confident that all was well. The doctor looked at us and said his blood counts were very good.

I jokingly said, "I saw you taking a long time to look at his blood."

The doctor responded, "I thought I saw something, but I didn't. I double-checked, and all is well."

I know I had the biggest smile imaginable on my face.

Time passed, and Seanny was now in second grade. He had his first show-and-tell. He took this very seriously. He went through everything he owned, trying to figure out what to take in. Then he knew. He wanted to take his mediport to show his class. I got permission from his teacher first. I didn't want to gross out any of the kids or teachers. To this day, I think that might have been the most unique item ever brought in for show-and-tell. He explained to his class what his mediport was and what it was for. Little did I know that God was working out so many details. His teacher's aide, who was a middle-aged woman, was diagnosed with terminal cancer a few weeks after this show-and-tell presentation. Seanny came home and told me about her, so we decided to pray for her and send her flowers. She called our home that night to thank us, and I got to tell her Seanny's story. She said she was very encouraged and asked us to continue praying. About a month later, she called and told us she was healed. Hallelujah!

Chapter 11

Over the next couple of years, God continued to teach me. I was so hungry for the word of God. Every time I thought I knew all there was to know, I realized I had just scratched the surface. My children were learning the ways of God, too. They would talk to Jesus just as easily as they talked to anyone else. God's grace and mercy were abundant in our lives. I was determined to teach my children not to fear. I told them there was nothing too big for our God to handle. Their wisdom, knowledge, and faith were mature well beyond their years. I couldn't be happier. My heart's desire was for my children to have a close personal relationship with Jesus. I wanted my children to see and love others the way Jesus did. And God was giving me the desires of my heart.

I remember Alysha came home from school one day complaining about a girl in her class. She told me this girl was a bully to everyone and was just plain mean. I sat Alysha down and told her when someone is really hurting about something, sometimes that person acts out in anger. I told my daughter that we needed to pray for this girl, so we did. I told Alysha to try to be nice to her even when she was at her meanest.

A few days later, Alysha came home from school looking very sad. I asked her what was wrong. She said she had been nice to this girl for the past few days. That day the whole class got to play in the gym, which was a real treat. This girl sat down on the side. Alysha went over to her and asked if she was going to play. She said she couldn't. Her foster parents wouldn't buy her sneakers. You needed those types of shoes to play in the gym. Alysha then realized what a hard life this girl had. So now my daughter was feeling really bad. I told her she could be either sympathetic or compassionate. Alysha asked me what the difference was. I told her if she was sympathetic toward this girl, then she would feel sorry for her. If she chose to be compassionate, she would do something about it. I told her Jesus always chose compassion. Alysha told me she wanted to be compassionate. She ran upstairs to her bedroom to get all the money she had. I knew it wasn't quite enough to get a pair of shoes, but I told her I'd make up the difference. So we went to the store and bought this girl a pair of shoes. I told Alysha it was very wrong to lie, but maybe we could make up a story so this girl wouldn't think she was a charity case, because she wasn't. Alysha told the girl she had a pair of shoes she got as a gift that didn't fit her. She wanted her to have them. Alysha said the girl was so happy.

The next day, I got a call from Alysha's teacher. He wanted to know if this girl had bullied a pair of sneakers off my daughter. I explained the situation to him but told him to tell no one. I was so proud of my girl and her generous heart.

My children cared about others so much. They would give up their food, clothes, and money to anyone who had a need. One year at Seanny's school Christmas party, the kids had a gift exchange. Boys bought a gift for a boy, and girls bought a gift for a girl. Seanny received a Pokémon gift from a boy. Even though it was so popular, I didn't allow my kids to play with those. He thanked the boy and figured he would secretly get rid of it at home. Well, there was a very poor girl in Seanny's class who also had a weight problem. One of the girls received her gift, which was a generic bottle of bubble bath. Some of the girls said, "Ew, that's awful."

Seanny said the girl looked so sad.

So he went to the girl who received the bubble bath and said, "Would you mind trading with me? My mom would love to have bubble bath."

The girl gladly exchanged gifts with Seanny. The poor girl came over to Seanny, smiling. She was glad that I would like the gift. When Seanny told me the story, my heart just melted. That was an extremely special gift that I cherished. Again, I could see God at work through my children.

Seanny had to go have a complete physical, which included blood work, an EKG, and other tests. They said the majority of children who take the amount of chemotherapy that Seanny did have some bad side effects. Some children have heart problems, others have learning problems, and still others have slower reflexes. There were various bad side effects that they were checking for. After his checkup exam and tests were over with, we waited for the results. The doctor came in reading a folder full of papers that were Seanny's. He proceeded to tell us that Seanny was in the minority that didn't have any bad side effects from his chemo treatments. He was very healthy. My mind immediately thought of the story in Luke chapter 17. There were ten lepers who came to Jesus asking to be healed. Jesus told them to go show themselves to the priest. On their way there, they were healed. One of the men who had been cured of leprosy came back to Jesus and fell at His feet, thanking Him.

Jesus said to the man, "Were not all ten healed? Has only one come back? Rise up and go; your faith has made you whole."

I believe all ten men were healed, but the one who came back was made whole. I believe he didn't have any scars or remains of leprosy. His grateful spirit got him full restoration. We were like the one who came back. Seanny had no bad effects from his chemo. He was not only healed but made whole. Until the day God calls me home to be with Him, I will always be like the one who came back to thank and praise Jesus for all that He's done.

As the years passed, life seemed to be going by rather smoothly. I got a job teaching preschool at a Christian school. The schedule allowed me to put my children on the bus in the morning and be there before they came home from school. It also allowed me to help in a small way with our finances. Most of all, I got to share God's word and love with the children and their families.

Things weren't perfect, but they weren't crazy either. Sean and I still had our ups and downs. Financially, we were still digging ourselves out of a hole. But we were all healthy, the kids were doing great in school, and Sean and I both had good jobs. I was content.

In 2004, I took my girls to see the movie *The Passion of the Christ* when it came out. Seanny wasn't quite ten years old, so I thought he was still too young to see it. As we sat in the theater, the movie came on. The first thing that played on the big screen was Isaiah 53:5, our favorite verse on healing. I got choked up just seeing that Bible verse in a public movie theater. This was the hardest movie I had ever watched. It was pretty much nonstop torture of

Jesus. When it came to the scene where they were whipping Jesus, I had tears pouring down my face. Because Jesus willingly allowed that whip to tear open the flesh on His back and body, my son was healed. I kept whispering, "Thank you, Jesus…thank you, Jesus," the whole time.

When it got to the scene where they nailed Jesus to the cross and raised Him up on it to hang there and die, the Lord said to my spirit, "And that's why your family and you are forgiven and saved."

I was completely overwhelmed at how much Jesus went through for us and how hard it must have been for God the Father to see His Son go through this. As Jesus hung on that cross, He didn't even look human. His body was torn, ripped apart, and bleeding. A crown of thorns had been shoved deep into His head. He had huge spikes nailed into His hands and feet. He hung naked on that cross, bearing our guilt and shame. He did all of this to take our punishment. He got what we deserved. Every sin—past, present, and future—was laid upon Him. He went through this so we wouldn't have to. As His sinless blood dripped from His body, I thought of the New Covenant that Jesus provided for us. Salvation was no longer based on our performance and works but solely on what Jesus did. His perfect blood was shed for the remission of our sins. The Creator dying for His creation. No longer do we have to cover up our sins through works and sacrifices. Jesus's blood washed away our sins completely.

My love for Jesus took on such a deeper meaning. I had read about what Jesus went through for me many times, but seeing it was completely different. We as humans tend to be visual creatures. Watching the crucifixion helped me understand just how far Jesus went for us. He could have stopped this humiliation, torture, and insanity at any moment. Jesus said, "Don't you know I could call ten legions [ten thousand] of angels to destroy the world and set myself free?"

But He didn't. He did not want us to be separated from God any longer. He knew sin could not stand in the presence of the Holy God. God wanted His family back. So Jesus bore the sin of the world, taking on our punishment, so we could be reunited with God. When Jesus said, "It is finished," He wasn't talking about His life. He meant all the requirements of the Old Testament law had been fulfilled. Every prophecy had been accomplished. The New Covenant had been established, the new and perfect Covenant. Once we ask Jesus to be our Lord and Savior, we become coheirs with Him. Everything He has, we have. We didn't deserve this sacrifice. We didn't deserve to be forgiven. We didn't deserve Jesus's mercy and grace. You can't earn it, work for it, or be good enough for it. But it's there for us; it's a free gift to anyone who will receive it. How absolutely, incredibly amazing!

Finally, Seanny had his ten-year checkup and blood work done. He was almost thirteen years old.

When the doctor came into our room with the results, he looked me straight in the eyes and said, "I will finally agree with you. Your son is cured and cancer-free."

I was smiling from head to toe. Inside I was doing cartwheels and back-flips. God is good. Always.

Of course, this was another reason for a celebration. I believe God enjoys it when His children have fun and celebrate. We decided to throw Seanny a surprise thirteenth birthday/healed-of-cancer party. Sean had bought him a very old, very pathetic-looking, beat-up 1984 Monte Carlo when he was twelve. I think he paid one hundred dollars for it. The plan was to restore it for him when he turned sixteen. They stored it in my parents' barn in the meantime. Well, Sean and a few other guys thought it would be a great idea to restore the car for Seanny's surprise party. Sean loved to race his 1965 Chevy Impala, and Seanny loved to go watch him. They figured if they restored the Monte Carlo, Seanny could race it in the junior racing bracket. The party was five weeks away. That was very little time to accomplish this task, a complete and total restoration inside and out.

We've never liked the word "impossible." So, besides going to work, Sean spent all his time working on Seanny's car at his friend's garage. I snuck down as much as possible to see the incredible progress. When Seanny asked his dad why he was always busy and never home, Sean told him that he was building a huge A-frame swing for the girls.

About three and a half weeks into the project, Seanny came into my room to talk to me. He looked so sad and serious.

He said, "Mom, I think Dad is cheating on you."

Shocked and surprised, I said, "What gives you that idea?"

He said, "It should only take Dad a few days to build the girls a swing frame. He's been gone 'round the clock for weeks, supposedly working on it. What else could he be doing?"

I tried so hard not to laugh.

I said to him, "Seanny, I've been down to see what Dad is working on. It's really a much bigger project than you realize. I am positive that he is not cheating on me. I think he'll be done in less than two weeks now."

Then I gave Seanny a big hug and told him not to worry. Poor thing, he was so concerned about me.

The day of the party finally arrived. It was a beautiful, hot, sunny day. Sean had the party going in full swing. I took Seanny and the girls out to eat. I said we should take Dad something to eat over at the police lodge because he was working there. As we pulled up in the long driveway, Seanny asked why there were so many cars there. Everyone was waiting for him and shouted, "Happy birthday!"

Seanny was so surprised. He asked why his dad's car trailer was parked outside. I told him Sean had brought a car for him to take a ride in. Seanny figured it was his dad's racecar and didn't think twice about it.

During the party, a friend of ours made a video for the song "Who Am I?" with pictures of the past thirteen years of our family. He played it for everyone to watch. It was a wonderful surprise and made me realize how far we had come. At the end of the video, it read: And by Jesus's stripes, Seanny is healed. Isaiah 53. Amen.

Finally it was time to take Seanny outside. When the trailer doors were opened, Sean backed out a very loud, very beautiful Chevy Monte Carlo. Seanny just looked at it. He had no idea this was his car fully restored.

His dad said, "What do you think?"

Seanny replied, "Whose is this?"

Sean said, "This is your car from Pappy's barn. This is what we have been working on nonstop for the past five weeks."

Seanny was speechless for a few minutes. Then a huge smile came across his face. It was exactly like the picture he drew of how he wanted it to be someday. It was silver and black with silver ghost flames going toward the back of the car. It had a new gray interior. On the back deck were the names of everyone who had helped with the car. It said "Survivor" above the car door, and on the trunk it read: No weapon formed against me shall prosper. Isaiah 54:17. It had a ratchet shifter and Bose speakers just like he dreamed of. So many people helped and voluntarily donated to make this project happen. Sean is so gifted with cars, and I was extremely proud of the job he had done. Then people had gotten together and bought Seanny an official racing suit and gear. It was like a dream come true for him.

When Sean took him for a ride, I don't know who was happier. They started the car up, and it had such a loud rumble to it. Someone had donated an amazing Flow Master dual exhaust system for it. They drove off down the road together. They were only gone a few minutes, but it gave me time to think about all God had done for us. Seanny was celebrating his thirteenth birthday/ten-year mark. Some thought we'd never see this day. God told me differently. I'm so glad I chose to believe Him.

Sean & My Wedding 7-7-90

Brittini (back), Alysha & Seanny 1996

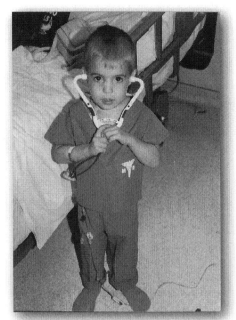

Seanny in Children's Hospital 1997

Seanny "My Bald Eagle" 1998

Seanny opening *The Relay for Life* 1998

Seanny's Remission Party 1998

Our family singing at Christmas – Brittini, Sean, Alysha, Seanny & me

"Sean's Super Sports" – Alysha, Sean, me, Seanny & Brittini

"Scott Racing" – Brittini, Seanny, Alysha, Sean & me (and our dogs Dixie & Daisy)

"Alysha's Wedding" – Ray, Brittini, me, Sean, Alysha, Chris & Seanny

Chapter 12

$\mathcal{L}$ife continued. The kids were growing and getting older. They were very involved in their church youth group, school activities, sports, and music. They were all involved in our church's praise and worship team. Brittini played the violin or guitar, Alysha Rae sang, and Seanny played the bass. God was placing a call on Brittini's heart to get involved with mission groups. Sean and I felt she was still too young to leave the country. I figured with time, she would change her mind regarding this. I couldn't have been more wrong.

When Brittini was sixteen years old, she got pretty sick. She had no energy and just didn't feel right. She had a lump on her neck, which I figured was a swollen lymph node due to an infection. After a couple of days, I took Brittini to a medical center to be checked. They drew some blood to be tested and told us to take her home and have her rest. My mom came over to sit with her one day so I could go back to work. I had been calling off to stay with her, but since she slept most of the day, I decided I'd better go back. I got a phone call from the clinic while I was still at work. They told me I should take Brittini to Children's Hospital to be checked. They said her platelets were very low, and her hemoglobin was even lower. I went cold. I knew what those counts meant. I asked them what they thought was wrong, but they wouldn't say.

I said, "Listen, I had a son who had leukemia years ago. I know what those counts should be and why. Tell me what you think is going on."

They said, "We are almost positive your daughter has cancer."

I hung up the phone and could feel myself fighting the tears. This couldn't be happening again. Lightning isn't supposed to hit the same place twice. I didn't want my daughter to go through this. I didn't want to go through it again. I left work immediately and headed home. On the way, I talked to God.

"Okay, Lord, I know that You provided healing for Brittini just like you did for Seanny. I know nothing is impossible for You. I know that You are able and willing to take care of her better than I can. I know this isn't Your will for her and that You didn't cause this. If we have to go through years of chemotherapy again, we will. I give You permission to be in control of the outcome," I said with a shaky voice.

"My child, I have taught you so much. Your faith is great. Take a stand. Take authority. Use My word. Trust Me," God spoke to my spirit.

When I arrived home, I told my mom what was going on. Then I called Sean to explain the situation and told him I was leaving right away to take her to the hospital. Sean asked me to wait for him so he could go with us. I called Brittini into the living room and told her the doctors were concerned about her and had told us to take her to Children's Hospital. I didn't tell Brittini what they suspected. I wasn't going to instill fear into my daughter. My mom and I anointed her with oil and prayed over her. I claimed that by Jesus's stripes, Brittini was healed. Sean arrived home, and off to Children's Hospital we went.

Sean was very quiet on the drive there. Brittini and I were singing praise songs to God. Satan kept reminding me about the same trip we made many years ago on those roads. He kept saying in my head, "It's happening again."

I knew he was trying to fill my husband's head with the same lies. I got righteously angry this time. I knew my God well at this point. I knew what to expect from Him. I knew what He provided for us. I knew what to do. I told Satan to shut up. I rebuked fear in the name of Jesus. As always, God gave me His peace that passes all understanding.

We arrived at the hospital, and they took us back to an exam room immediately. The doctors told Sean and me that according to the reports they were looking at and because of the lump in her neck, the doctors we had talked to at home were probably correct. They took more blood from Brittini and started doing a checkup. The lump started going away as they were examining her. The doctors looked baffled. The blood results came back absolutely fine. They said to take her home; she might have had a virus, but nothing serious was wrong.

Brittini asked me if they had thought she had cancer. I told her, "Yes, that was what we were told." She asked why we didn't tell her.

I said, "I didn't want to speak it out until we were sure. I didn't want to put fear in you."

Her reply was, "It would have been no big deal. If I had it, I would have been healed. What's the worst possible outcome? I die? It's a win-win situation no matter what. Going to Heaven is not a consolation prize. Besides, God had showed me this in a dream. I had peace about it."

My kids—not even death could scare them.

Now some might say the first lab reports were wrong or that the doctors had just misdiagnosed her. But I know that I had witnessed a miracle.

Someone once said, "Satan attacks what he fears." Wow, we must really scare him. We were becoming his worst nightmare. It says in Revelation 12:11, "They [God's children] overcame him [Satan] by the blood of the Lamb and the words of their testimony."

That is so powerful. Jesus, the perfect Lamb of God, shed His blood for us. His blood is power. Our words, our testimonies, are powerful. Put the two together, and you'll whoop the devil every time!

Since Brittini was sixteen years old, we decided to let her go on her first mission trip. A group from our church was going to Honduras. Brittini really wanted to go, and Sean and I could feel God's calling on her life. It was a ten-day trip that cost around three thousand dollars. We told her if she could come up with the money, we'd permit her to go.

She smiled and said, "That's fine. God will provide."

And He did. She came home a changed young lady. She now knew her call was in the mission field.

As I have said, I was a very protective mother. I allowed my children to have fun and explore life; I just wasn't far away. I knew God was protecting them, but I also believe He used me as one of those sources. I didn't want them to have to go through any of the pain I had gone through. I would always have their backs.

There was a situation in which my children were involved that caused Sean and me some concern. I talked to a man of God about it, and I was shocked at his response. Unfortunately, he knew some of our past. So somehow the conversation went from Sean and me being concerned about our children's safety to how people wouldn't want their children around me if they knew how I really was. This man knew that Sean and I had some marital problems, but that was it. We had worked through our difficulties. Why was he saying such mean things to me? As he was putting me down, all my past failures, mistakes, and abuse came to my mind. I could feel the pain and shame overcoming me. Tears started flowing. I immediately put the wall back up that shielded me from the world. Would my past ever quit haunting me? This whole conversation started because I was concerned about my children's safety. How had it gotten to this point?

As I was driving home, the voice of lies was talking loud and clear. Men had hit me because I deserved it. I had been taken advantage of because I was worthless. I wasn't always good enough for my husband. I had murdered my own child. The man of God confirmed it; people wouldn't like me if they really knew me. I withdrew from people after this conversation. Sure, I put up a good front, but I wasn't letting anyone get close. I would not be trusting anyone; my heart couldn't take it. I understood God's grace and mercy, but I didn't comprehend His love.

Chapter 13

*I*t was May 2008. I didn't see it coming, but another storm was about to hit our family. My dad had been having severe heartburn. When we asked him how long it had been going on, he said over ten years. My dad was a private man and never complained. He had to have an endoscopy done. He wouldn't have told anyone about it, but he wasn't allowed to drive home after the test. My mom took him to the hospital for the procedure. Before he even woke up from the test, the doctor informed my mother that he had esophagus cancer. My mom called me immediately at work and asked me to come to the hospital. I left as soon as I hung up the phone. Oh no, not my dad. He had already been healed of cancer twice.

I pulled it together. I had to be strong for my mom and him. As my dad was waking up, he asked what was wrong. I wasn't there before he went under, and now I was. He knew something was up. I told him the doctor said he had cancer. I told him not to worry about it, that everything was going to be fine. He took the news well, but I could tell by his eyes that he was concerned. He would never express it in front of my mom, though. We didn't say much; I knew we'd get to talk as soon as we got a chance to be alone.

My dad went back to work the next day. My parents were celebrating their fortieth anniversary that month, so my sister and I were talking about doing something special for them. She thought it would be fun if our brother and his family, her and her family, and me and my family got together and took my parents to Hershey Park for a long weekend. I thought that sounded like a great idea. She said she'd check into it and get back to me.

My dad stopped at my house on his way home from work. I told him the kids weren't home from school yet, and he said that was okay because he needed to talk to me. I told him about our plans to go to Hershey, and he said not to make any reservations. I just looked at him. I could sense he was trying to tell me something.

After stammering for a couple of minutes, he finally said, "I went to the doctors. I have to have surgery; if I don't, I will die soon. If I have the surgery, I still might die. The recovery time after this surgery takes months, sometimes years. I want you to know I've had a good life. I don't have any regrets. My children and grandchildren are all saved. I am ready to go home to be with the Lord. I don't want you worrying, and I don't want to tell the rest of the family any more details than what's necessary. I don't mean to put so much on you, but you're strong."

I felt like the breath of life had just been sucked out of me. I refused to let myself cry. If I did then my dad wouldn't confide in me; he'd be worried I couldn't handle it. *Stay strong*, I told myself.

"Dad, you can beat this. You've seen what God can do. I will be with you through it all, and I expect to hear the truth about everything," I said to him.

He said he'd better head home so my mom wouldn't wonder where he was. He thanked me and then said, "I love you."

"I love you, too, Dad," I replied.

Our family was never good with words. In the past twenty years, I think my dad had told me three times that he loved me. I was okay with that. Now the grandkids were a different matter. He was always telling them he loved them. It was so sweet.

As I shut the door when my dad left, I was overwhelmed with sadness. I started crying harder than I ever had in my life. I couldn't seem to catch my breath. I went to the bathroom and was sick to my stomach. I couldn't stop. I was getting angry with myself for having this reaction, but something down deep told me my dad wasn't going to be with me much longer. My dad wasn't perfect, but he was a person I could confide in. He could keep a secret better than anyone I knew. He was like a second father to my children. I needed him.

Sean came home about thirty minutes after my dad left. He came upstairs to change out of his work clothes and saw me sitting on the bathroom floor.

"What's wrong with you?" he asked.

I rarely lost control, and he could tell I was there.

"My dad was here a little bit ago. He told me he was at the doctor's office today. I need to talk to you," I said softly.

"Some guys are coming over to work in the garage. They'll be here soon. We'll have to talk later," he said and quickly left the room.

Now I was angry instead of sad. How often had I told Sean I really needed him in the past eighteen years? Maybe three or four times total. And this was the response I got each time. Couldn't he ever be there for me?

I got myself under control before the kids came home from school. I told them a little bit about Pappy without going into detail, and I told them to be praying. I knew God could work a miracle. I couldn't understand why I felt so hopeless down deep. I had no one to talk to and felt so alone.

Later that night, after the kids went to bed, Sean finally came up from the garage to our bedroom. It was dark, and I was staring at the ceiling. The only light was from the moon shining through our window. He sat down next to me.

After a few minutes of silence, he said, "I'm sorry I left you alone when you needed to talk. I knew what you were going to say, and I couldn't handle it. For one thing, I hate to see you hurting. The other is your dad has been a dad to me, too. He has taken a bigger interest in me and cared about me more than my own family. I can't stand the thought of him not being here."

I didn't say anything. Sean lay down next to me and put his arm around me. I could feel the tears coming again. Sometimes there are no words to be spoken. My heart was broken in a thousand pieces. I couldn't imagine life without my dad. He was always there.

Halfway through the night, I snuck out of bed and went to our living room. I needed to talk to God.

"Lord, I know that it's Your will for my dad to be healed. I know You can make this right. Why do I feel this way?"

The Lord spoke gently to my spirit: "This is different than with Seanny. You stood in the gap for him and spoke life. It was your decision what to believe and claim. Although you can stand in the gap for your dad, the outcome is his decision."

I asked the Lord to give me strength. I knew my dad really needed me for the first time ever. He would confide in me, and if I couldn't handle it, he would talk to no one. My dad hated to burden people. He hated to see anyone worried or scared. I had to be strong. I had to stay in control. My dad tried to be there for all of us; now it was my turn to be there for him.

It was now June 2008. My parents picked me up at my house around four thirty in the morning. We were headed to a hospital in Pittsburgh, where my dad was going to have surgery to have his esophagus removed. It would be at least a seven-hour surgery. As we pulled into the parking garage, I made a mental note of where my dad was parking the car. I knew I'd be driving my mom home later, and neither of us ever remembered where we parked. I helped my dad sign in and go through the countless papers and forms. After about twenty minutes of paperwork, my dad and I returned it all to the receptionist. They told him they needed a person to contact in an emergency. He gave them my name and number and told them to only contact me.

A nurse came out and led us to a prep room. They explained again what was involved in the surgery. They told us we had about five minutes with my dad before they had to take him to the operating room. My mom and I prayed with him and told him we loved him. I remember making a couple of jokes with him, trying to ease the atmosphere. Then they took him away. My mom and I went to the waiting room together. We found some drinks and sat down on the couch. I told her to get comfortable because it was going to be a long day.

After about an hour, she closed her eyes. I don't know if she was actually asleep or not, but I pulled a book from my backpack and started reading. I inherited the love of books from my father. On average, I read at least two books a week. I could get lost in a book and be oblivious to everything around me.

After a few hours, our pastor showed up in the waiting room. He came to keep us company and to pray with us. My dad had been in surgery for about three hours, so we decided to grab a quick lunch. We knew he'd be at least four more hours, so I told the nurse we'd be back shortly and to call if they needed anything.

I wasn't really hungry, but if I didn't eat, neither would my mom. Our pastor helped get my mom's mind off of her fears. He stayed with us for about three and a half hours, which I greatly appreciated. When he left, I went to the nurse's station and asked if she knew how much longer before my dad was done in surgery. She told us they would let us know when he was in recovery.

Finally, after about nine hours in surgery, they told us my dad was in recovery, and we could see him shortly. I think the nurses were taking pity on us for being there so long, so they took us back to see him sooner than they should have. We walked into his room, and he was just starting to come out of the anesthesia. His words were muffled and did not make sense. He hadn't been cleaned up yet, so there was blood all over him. You could see where they had just freshly cut him open. My mother panicked and started crying. I quickly walked over to my dad and told him we loved him and were praying for him. I told him I needed to take Mom home, and I would see him in the morning. He nodded, and I very gently hugged him good-bye. I had to get my mom out of there. I knew my dad wouldn't remember much about that evening, but my mom would.

As we got into the car and headed home, I tried to explain to my mother that he would be a lot different the next day. He would be talking clearly and would be bandaged and cleaned up. It made her feel a little better but not much. She decided she wanted to spend the night at my house, so we stopped by her home first to get what she needed. Alysha was fifteen and working at the local ice cream shop. I told my mom we could stop there to grab a bite to eat and then take Alysha home with us. I had to get my mom's mind off what she had just seen. It was an awful picture to have stuck in her head. Believe me, I knew.

I tried to keep the mood light the rest of the night. My mind kept flashing back to how my dad was when we left him. It wasn't a pretty sight. Thankfully, my mom fell asleep quickly. I lay there, talking to God. I prayed for my dad. My heart ached, but I wouldn't allow myself to have a pity party. I was needed, and I took that job seriously.

Early the next morning, I got up and got ready to go to the hospital. The drive took about an hour. My dad was still in the intensive care unit. When the clock finally got to the time we were allowed back, my mom and I got up and waited by the door. A nurse came and got us and walked us back to his room.

You see and hear so many strange sounds in a hospital, none of which are comforting. When we entered my dad's cubicle, he was awake. He was better than the last time we saw him but not much. He was cleaned up and had a huge bandage engulfing his chest and neck. Tubes were coming from various parts of his body. His voice was weak and raspy. You could tell by his eyes that he was in a lot of pain. We stood there for a moment, not knowing what to say or do.

Finally, I said, "Boy, you look better than you did yesterday. How are you feeling?"

"Okay" was about the only word he could get out.

I went over and sat down on a stool next to him. My mom gave him an easy hug and sat down on the other side of him. We were not used to seeing my dad this way. The nurse came in to check his vitals and put something in his IV. I asked her if there was anything we needed to know. She said he was doing as good as could be expected after the major surgery he just had. She patted my shoulder and left the room.

I wanted to ask my dad questions about how he was doing and what he remembered, but I didn't want him to strain to have to answer. So we sat there, holding his hands. My mom would make an occasional comment. He kept drifting off to sleep on us. I just wanted him to relax and to be out of pain. We weren't allowed to stay long. I told my dad I would see him tomorrow. I knew he wouldn't remember much about that day either.

I took my mom to her house and headed home. I had chores to catch up on, and I needed to spend time with my family. I called the hospital about every other hour to check up on my dad. Thankfully, he was sleeping most of the time. He needed the rest.

The next morning, I decided to go to the hospital by myself. I wanted to talk to the medical staff and get some answers about how my dad was really doing. I was about to leave when I heard my phone ringing.

The voice on the other end said, "May I please speak to Tracey Scott?"

"This is she," I replied.

"This is one of your father's nurses. He's okay, but he suffered a heart attack. You are the name to contact in an emergency," she said.

"I thought his heart was strong. What happened?"

"His heart is strong. The surgery was very invasive and put a lot of stress on his heart and organs," she answered.

"I'm leaving right now. I'll be there in about an hour," I said.

I didn't know what to do. Should I call my family? Our pastor? Knowing my dad, I figured he wouldn't want me to call anyone. Great. This was making a hard situation even tougher. I decided I would go see him and let him make the decision about who to tell.

On the drive to Pittsburgh, I had a lot of time to pray. I told God I really needed Him to guide me on every problem and situation that arose. I didn't want to disappoint my dad, and I wanted to protect my family from some of the grimness of what it's like to deal with cancer. I had already been through it. I had heard so many negative, dreadful reports that I knew how to filter out what I should and shouldn't tell people. I didn't want anyone to have to carry that burden; it's too heavy.

I arrived at the hospital and hurriedly made it to my dad's room. I was supposed to wait for a nurse to escort me in, but I didn't care. They could escort me out if they could catch me. My dad was asleep, so I quietly went over and touched his hand. He opened his eyes and looked at me.

He gave a small smile and said, "That was quick."

"I didn't know how serious it was. I didn't know if you needed me to pray for your healing or call you back from the dead," I said with an even bigger smile.

My dad had passed his sense of humor on to me, for which I am grateful.

"I'll be fine. It was only a heart attack. You can pray with me, though," he replied jokingly.

After we prayed, they wanted to run some tests on him. I told him I'd wait in the lobby until they were done. He seemed better than the day before, although he was still so weak and in nonstop pain. He was on an IV. They had told us he couldn't eat solid foods for over six weeks. He would be sent home with a feeding tube in his stomach. My dad had always been on the thin side, so I was praying he wouldn't lose too much weight.

It didn't take long for my dad to return to his room. The nurse said his heart looked fine. They were amazed at how quickly and wholly his body was recovering. My dad was a firm believer in the power of words. He said he'd be fine, and he was.

Throughout the next two months, my days were the same: take care of my family, visit my dad, check on my mom, come home and do chores, and spend time with my family. I was being pulled in so many directions. In one way, that was good. It didn't give me much time to sit and think about everything going on. On the other hand, I was wearing thin. I was only one person.

My dad was finally released and ready to come home. *This will make my life easier*, I thought. *They only live about ten minutes away, so I'll have a lot more time now.* I couldn't have been more wrong.

My dad needed so much care. He had so many bandages on his chest and back that needed to be changed at least two times a day. He needed to have all seventeen of his incisions cleaned multiple times a day. He needed food hooked up to his feeding tube. On and on and on the list went. So I would go help my dad and mom at least twice a day and more if necessary. My poor dad was allergic to the medical tape that was holding his bandages on. His skin was so raw and sore. He was such a good patient, though. Every time I would pull a bandage off, part of his skin would come off with it. He never complained about the inconveniences or pain.

The next seven months were difficult. My dad's feeding tube was constantly getting blocked and infected. He had absolutely no appetite, which caused him to lose weight rapidly. Pain was his companion around the clock. The chemotherapy and radiation were taking their toll on his body. He was in the ER or hospital almost as much as he was home. Death was standing at the door.

I looked at my dad one day as he was sleeping. He was six-foot-one and weighed 125 pounds. How much could a human body take? Sometimes I wish he would get angry, complain, or cry. Something! My dad was determined to stay strong and in control. He was beating the odds at every turn. I could tell he was getting tired of the fight, though. The doctor's reports were sinking in. He was making comments about not being around in a year.

Even though it was hard, I was so glad my dad allowed me to be with him at every appointment, ER visit, and hospital stay. I was hearing every report he was hearing. He would let down around me. On one trip to the hospital, he moaned and gasped the whole time. It was so hard seeing him in so much pain. How did he hide how severe it was from the rest of the family?

Almost nine months after his initial surgery, my dad was in so much pain that I insisted they figure out what was wrong. They kept telling us it takes time to heal from his original surgery. I knew better. They decided to do surgery to reinsert his feeding tube and to see if there was anything else wrong. He now weighed around 112 pounds. I sat in the waiting room by myself for hours. The doctor finally called me back to the conference room. He asked if anyone else was with me, and I said no. He sighed and told me to have a seat. I could feel the butterflies in my stomach.

The doctor said, "Your dad came through surgery fine and is in a recovery room. We were unable to put his feeding tube back in because he is so full of cancer. That's why he's in so much pain. You need to get all his things in order. He has six weeks or less to live."

I just looked at the doctor for a couple of minutes. I knew that if I talked, I would cry, and I refused to do that.

I took a deep breath and said, "My dad doesn't need to hear this report. Let me choose what to tell him. Thank you for doing your best."

The doctor said with tears in his eyes, "Is there anything I can do for you?"

"Actually, there is. I know after surgery I usually have to wait an hour or two to see him. My son has a school orchestra concert tonight that I'd hate to miss. Can you let me see him now for a few minutes?"

"Come on," the doctor said. "I'll make an exception and take you back personally."

I gratefully followed him back. My dad was awake but a little groggy. The doctor left us alone.

"What did they find out?" my dad asked.

"Well, you have some more cancer in you. The feeding tube wasn't a good idea right now," I said quietly.

"Tracey, I knew this was coming. I am tired of fighting. I want to go home to be with the Lord. I know this is hard on you. I appreciated you always being here for me, staying strong in front of me. Break this easily to the family. This is the last time I'm coming to the hospital. My fight is over, but I still won."

I leaned over and kissed my dad.

"You are a great man. I can't tell you what you mean to me," I whispered.

My dad just smiled at me.

"Don't you have an orchestra concert to get to?"

"There will be more of those. I would rather sit here with you."

I smiled back sadly.

"Don't be silly. Your son needs you even more than I do. I'll be here in the morning, waiting for you to take me home," he said.

"Okay, Dad. If you need anything, call me. I love you," I said.

As I was walking down the hallway to get to the parking garage, I found a little alcove from which to call my family. Suddenly I didn't want to call anyone. Why was I there alone? Why did I have to hear the worst news of my life by myself? Why did I always have to be the strong one? Why was I always alone? Why couldn't I fall apart just once and have someone comfort and encourage me? Why, why, why? I was so sad and angry at the same time.

Suddenly my Lord was speaking to me. "Child, you've never been alone. I have always been right beside you. When your hearts breaks, so does Mine. Talk to Me; I will listen and comfort you."

"Oh, God," I sobbed. "I want my dad to be healed. I want him to be around for a long, long time."

"It's not up to you, my child. Your dad wants to come home; allow him to," God said.

"Oh, Lord, I still need him," I cried brokenheartedly.

"It will be a temporary separation in the light of eternity. And *I Am* more than enough for what you need," He said tenderly.

"Okay, Lord. I trust You."

And with that simple statement, I surrendered.

After the concert that night, I talked to my entire family. I told them Dad was coming home the next day and that the doctor said he had less than six weeks to live. They took the news hard but weren't overly surprised.

Sean went to the hospital with me the next day to pick up my dad. He was having a hard time walking, and I thought I might physically need help. When we arrived, there was a social worker who wanted to talk to me first. She asked if I wanted to take my dad to the Donnell House instead of home. The Donnell House is for people who don't have much time to live. I said absolutely not. The social worker proceeded to tell me it was going to get even harder to take care of him. I didn't care; I could handle it. My dad took care of both of his parents until they died. He supported them and let them keep their dignity to the very end. And I was going to do the same for him. They insisted on letting hospice come and talk with us the next day, and I said that we'd talk to them.

My dad was so anxious to leave the hospital and get home. When they finally released him, he got in the wheelchair so they could escort him out. He would thank every doctor and nurse he passed for the wonderful job they did with him. My heart was breaking as he was saying his final good-byes to the medical staff.

We got him into my Suburban and headed on the hour-long drive home. Sean and my dad were in the front seat, and I was sitting in the middle row seat. I knew this would be the last car ride my dad ever took. I was taking in everything one last time with him.

When we pulled into his driveway, he got out and practically ran into the house. He was so glad to be home. We got him settled inside and told him we were going to pick up his prescriptions and that we'd be back shortly.

That night, when I got home, I was exhausted. I had to work a few hours the next day and then we were going to my dad's to meet with hospice and then celebrate my grandma's eightieth birthday. My plate was too full. I finally drifted off to sleep, and my alarm was buzzing before I knew it.

When Sean, the kids, and I arrived at my parents' house, my mom was setting up for my grandma's party. The only people invited were my brother and his kids, my sister and her husband and kids, and my family. We wanted to celebrate my grandma's birthday and also spend time with my dad together.

After the party, everyone was in the living room with my dad. He was lying on the couch, just exhausted. His voice was getting weaker, and he was drifting off to sleep frequently. When it was time to leave, all the grandkids lined up to tell their Pappy good-bye. He gave each one of them his famous line that he always did—"Pappy loves you to pieces"—and hugged every one of them.

My sister and I were in the hallway getting ready to go home.

She said to me, "Dad is going home tonight. I just feel it."

I looked at her for a moment and said, "Then I'm staying here."

I told Sean I felt the need to spend the night. I told my mom to go to bed, and I would stay downstairs with Dad. After everyone was in bed for the night, my dad and I started watching a movie together like we had so many times before. He was drifting in and out of sleep. At around one o'clock in the morning, I went to sleep, too. I heard my dad stirring shortly after 3:00 a.m. I went over and asked him if he needed pain medicine.

"Up," was all he said.

By that time, I knew he was too weak to get up. I knew in my spirit that it was time for my dad to go home.

"Dad," I choked out a whisper. "It's okay to go home now."

"I am," he said, looking up. "Don't you see Him?"

Oh my, I knew my dad was seeing Jesus. His spirit was ready, but his body hadn't given up yet. And I knew why.

"Hold on, Dad," I said. "I'll go get Tommy."

I ran upstairs to get my brother. He hadn't accepted the fact that my dad was dying.

I knocked on the door and said, "Tommy, Dad wants to get up, and I need your help."

I didn't really need his help. My dad weighed 111 pounds. I could handle him myself, but I needed Tommy to tell Dad good-bye.

Tommy came downstairs, and something in his spirit told him my dad was leaving soon. He sat down next to our father and started hugging him. I heard him talking quietly, saying things that needed to be said. My mom had heard us moving around, and she came downstairs, too.

She sat down next to my dad and started hugging him. She told him she loved him and that he wasn't done being her husband after forty years.

She said, "You are my husband for eternity. It's okay to go home now, Tom."

Then she went to make some tea and coffee for us. Shortly after 6:00 a.m., I heard Tommy tell my dad it was okay to go home. That's what he was waiting for. At 6:55 a.m. on March 5, 2009, my dad left this world and entered Heaven. I know Jesus was waiting there to welcome him home. And because I had two children in Heaven, I knew he would get to be a pappy up there, too. He didn't know that, so I knew he had some special surprises waiting there for him. That gave me such peace.

I had prayed I would be with my dad when he died. God granted that request. I called Sean to tell him the news. He said the kids had just left for school, but he would go pick them up. They arrived at Pappy and Grandma's house about an hour later. Seanny walked in and gave me a hug. We found a letter that my dad had written to all of us back in his den. He had written it a few days before he died. It basically said that he loved us all, that he was very proud of us, and that God had given him way more than he deserved. He said he couldn't wait for us all to join him in Heaven. It would be a grand reunion!

The day of my dad's funeral was sunny but cool. Brittini played "Amazing Grace" on her violin. Then the grandkids and some of the youth group kids who called my dad Pappy sang a song. Sean gave the eulogy, which was so funny and inspirational. He talked about all the goofy things my dad did, and all the life lessons he taught us. Sean made my dad proud.

When we were saying our final good-byes at the gravesite, I didn't want to leave. I was the last to go. I knew my dad wasn't there, that he was celebrating up in Heaven, but I just didn't want to walk away.

Finally, I touched the casket and whispered, "I'll see you later, Dad."

I knew that a chapter of my life was over for now.

Chapter 14

*B*rittini was in her senior year of high school with only a couple of months left. She had been accepted into both the United States Air Force Academy and Messiah College. She was having a hard time deciding which place best suited her. After visiting the academy in Colorado, she decided to go there. So many people kept telling me I was crazy for allowing her to go into the military. "What if she ends up in Iraq or Saudi Arabia?" they would say.

In response to these positive comments, I would reply, "She's an adult and needs to make her own decisions. Besides, if God calls her to go to Iraq, then she's safer there than here at home."

Graduation day finally arrived. There were over 275 students in her graduating class. Brittini was one of the valedictorians. She had made straight A's from kindergarten through twelfth grade. We were so incredibly proud of her. She was the last to give her speech at the ceremony. When she got up to the podium, all I could think was how my dad would have loved to be there. She is such a gifted speaker. She talked for a minute or two and then her speech went directly to what was in her heart. She said it doesn't matter how much you know or what you accomplish in this life if Jesus isn't your Lord and Savior. She eloquently told everyone about Jesus's love for them. I was waiting for them to shut her microphone off. This was a public school, and Brittini wasn't just talking about God; she was talking about Jesus and salvation!

When she finished her speech, the applause was incredible. People got up out of their chairs and gave her a standing ovation. She was the only speaker to receive that.

God whispered to my heart, "Your dad could see her, and he heard her speech. She made us both proud." Smile.

Brittini went to the Air Force Academy and went through basic training. She excelled in every way. After she had been there for two months, I got a call from her. She asked if she could come home. I asked her if everything was all right.

She responded, "Yes, I like it here, but my heart is in the mission field. I want to go to Messiah College, where I can do what's really in my heart."

Of course I told her she could come home. God opened the doors for her to still get into Messiah College to start her freshman year and to still receive her scholarship. She enjoyed college to its fullest. It was about three and a half hours away from home, so I didn't get to see her as much as I would have liked to. In the second semester of her sophomore year, she got accepted to study abroad and do mission work in Thailand. She was beyond excited about this. She would be in Asia for five months. Even though I knew I'd miss her so much, I also knew this is what God put in her heart.

The Bible talks about the church being the body of Christ. It says we can't all be hands. We can't all be feet. We can't all be eyes. God calls each of us in different areas. Sometimes we think we should all feel the same way and do the same thing, but that is not what God says. Besides, that would be boring, and only one job would get done. So even though Sean and I never felt called to go to another country, we knew Brittini had. We also knew this was just the beginning.

I was determined to cover Brittini in prayer every day. I couldn't call or text her anytime I wanted. I had to wait until she was able to reach me. So every day I had to trust God and put her in His hands. One night I woke up feeling very uneasy. Brittini was in my heart, so I started praying for her. After a few minutes, the uneasy feeling was turning into fear. I kept on praying and declaring God's word over Brittini. The fear wouldn't go away.

Finally, I said, "Lord, what is it You are trying to tell me? What should I be interceding for?"

Sternly, like a loving Father, He said to me, "I will never use Satan's tools to try to tell you something. If you have fear, it is not from Me. Take authority over it and rebuke it."

I immediately said, "Fear, in the mighty name of Jesus, I rebuke you. I have God's peace that passes all understanding. I plead the precious blood of Jesus over Brittini. I am going to sleep now, and I am going to get the best rest I have ever had."

And that's just what I did. The fear left swiftly, and I went to sleep with no problem. I woke up feeling very rested and refreshed. The Lord taught me something that night. Every time there was an awful storm or tsunami in Thailand, I took authority over it and would claim a hedge of protection around Brittini. And I never feared. God is always ready to teach us something, and He never stopped amazing me. The greatest lesson God ever taught me was about to happen.

Chapter 15

As life continued, I never realized how heavy the burdens I carried had become. Even though life was good, and I was basically happy, there was always something holding me back. I was weary down deep in my soul. Wounds from the past thirty years were still unhealed. I wasn't satisfied anymore with just getting by and being content. I just couldn't put my finger on what was missing.

Every day, guilt, shame, and hurt would rear their ugly heads at me. As I was driving alone one day, I was feeling guilty about the abortion I had so many years before. So, of course, I started to repent. I was telling God how sorry I was for about the millionth time.

I heard God speak. He said, "Isn't what Jesus went through for you enough? Does He need to be whipped again? Should the thorns in His head have been longer? Was the cross not heavy enough? Should I make Jesus revisit hell?"

In shock, I asked, "Lord, what are You talking about?"

"Jesus paid the full price for your sins. He overpaid. He carried your guilt and shame. And when you asked Me to forgive you the first time, I removed your sins as far as the east is from the west. You're the only one holding that sin against you. I don't even remember it until you bring it back to My attention."

"Oh, Lord," I cried. "What You and Jesus provided is more than enough."

"Do you know the reason We did this for you? Because We love you. We love you more than all the stars in the sky. We love you more than all the sand on the seashores. The universe cannot hold all the love We have for you. You were *worth* the sacrifice. And We would do it all again if necessary."

And then…*God showed me His love.*

It washed over me like a tidal wave. I was completely consumed by His love. All my guilt, shame, and insecurities were washed away. My heart of stone just crumpled away. God gently tore down the walls and removed all the Band-Aids. He put in me His heart—a soft, gentle, perfect heart. In one moment of time, God restored me. The burdens I had carried for over thirty years were broken and shattered by the power of God's love. All the lies I believed ran away in fear at the power and intensity of God's love. God looked at me and saw my worth. I was His child. I know that complete and total restoration can take years, but God gave it to me in a second.

I was in love with God, totally head over heels in love. I felt like my heart was going to explode from the joy I was experiencing. Everything God had shown me and done for me over the years was simply because He loved me. God is love. I realized in that moment that I really did need a man to complete me: Jesus! I was worthy because Jesus said I was. In the Old Covenant, forgiveness was based upon striving and works. Man couldn't find rest or peace with God. On his own, man could never measure up. Nothing ever removed the sin; it just got covered up. God found fault with that covenant. He established the New Covenant, where everything is based upon Jesus's sacrifice. Jesus's blood completely annihilated sin. It's no longer about how good we are or if we earned forgiveness. We don't have to be perfect. We don't have to earn forgiveness and love. It's a gift—a free and simple gift. But it wasn't cheap; Jesus paid with His life. It just has to be received. Wow!

Because I had been forgiven, and God showed me His love, I could forgive everyone who ever hurt me. I hadn't realized how deeply rooted lies and bitterness had dug into me. When I allowed God to remove them, I felt love, His love, for everyone. It was just miraculous.

I began to see people the way God does. Instead of seeing an angry man who spoke harsh words, I saw a hurting man in need of God's love. When I heard women gossiping and putting people down, I saw women who were insecure and desperate for God's love. When I saw teenagers and young adults misusing their bodies, I saw people who only felt pain and needed God's healing and love. God's love changes every situation if you allow it to.

God showed me that I wasn't alone when it came to suffering and guilt. People were carrying burdens way too heavy for them, burdens God never intended for them to carry. God knew what each one of us would go though, and He provided the way to help us. His love isn't just some nice, fluffy thought. His love is power. It will break all bondages and heal every heart. It's more powerful than any drug and stronger than any addiction. God loves us fiercely and protectively.

The amazing thing about God's love is you don't have to earn or beg for it. He is offering it to everyone. You just have to accept it. There are no stipulations or conditions. Nothing you can do will cause God to withdraw it. But you can reject it. You can believe the lie that you don't deserve it or need it. But God is patiently waiting for you to receive it. Daddies are just that way.

Because of God's love, I started seeing Sean in a whole new way. The love I had for him seemed to multiply once I allowed God's love to overwhelm me. I hadn't realized how vehemently Satan opposed our marriage, how he tried to destroy it on so many levels. When Sean started seeing what God's love was doing in my life and that it was spilling over onto him, he started changing. God's love was healing our marriage. Sean was becoming the man God intended him to be. We aren't perfect, and we still have our disagreements. I am still one of the most stubborn people on the face of the earth with Sean as a close second. But it's different now; harsh words are hardly ever spoken, and forgiveness is asked for and received. There are no more walls. We have no need for boxes of Band-Aids. I am more in love with my husband now than I have ever been. That's the power of love.

Just when I thought God couldn't possibly bless me more, He surprised me. In the year 2013, I had more special events and memories than I could count. First, my son, Seanny, graduated from high school. As he walked across the stage to receive his diploma, I remembered when he was three years old, and I was told he might not live through the night. There he was, a grown man and graduating. He loves the Lord with all His heart. He is so intelligent. He is one of the most compassionate people I know, and he is one of the most protective people I know, too. He is gifted in so many areas, and I am excited to see how God is going to continue partnering with him for His glory. And to top it off, he treats me like a queen. Smile.

I believe God is going to use him in the healing ministry for starters. His passion is going to alter this world and point people to Jesus.

Second, Brittini married a man after God's own heart on July 7, 2013. They share the same anniversary as Sean and me. Ray Hill loves my daughter the way God intended a man to love a woman. He cherishes her and inspires her to follow God's will always. While they were on a mission trip to Israel, Ray proposed to Brittini by the Sea of Galilee. He has a heart for missions just like she does. He graduated from the United States Air Force Academy with honors. He is my son, not just by marriage but in my heart. Brittini is finishing up her bachelor's degree in biology, while Ray completes his graduate degree through the air force. Brittini is gifted in so many ways, too, and she is determined not to let anything God has given her go to waste. She ministers to others in every way imaginable. Together, they will change the world with God's love.

Then there's Alysha Rae, my Soappy. She graduated high school with honors and started attending college. In 2013, she met the man her heart would love forever. Christopher McConnell proposed to her, and she joyfully accepted. They were married on August 17, 2013. Christopher, too, is my son now. He had graduated college with a four-year degree in mechanical engineering. He treats my daughter like the princess she is, and together they are growing in God's love. Alysha is one of the most generous people this world has ever seen. She does a lot behind the scenes for God. She is always buying groceries, clothes, and gifts for people. Besides working a full-time job for a financial company, she also helps me with a Bible study. Together, she and Christopher are going to make an eternal difference in this world.

Last but not least, there's Sean, the one my heart loves. We have been through so much together. I have learned that love is not a feeling but a decision. We made a covenant before God, and we will be together through all of eternity. He has less than two years left until he retires from being a policeman. He has seen the ugly side of life, and he fights injustice daily. I am very proud of him and grateful for all the hard work he has done for our family.

We have always been able to laugh together, even in the worst circumstances. I have witnessed God softening his heart and am excited to see where God is taking him.

What about me? Well, I believed my first and only calling was to be a mother to my children. I put my entire heart and soul into it. I was determined to help my children grow into the adults God wanted them to be. I wasn't always the perfect example, but I spent many hours in prayer and standing in the gap for them. That is a calling I will have until we all get to Heaven. But my role is different now that they are adults. God isn't finished with me… He's just starting a new chapter. My dream is to own a large farm with a lot of land. I want it to be a retreat center where people will come to be healed, set free, and refreshed. I want to use all of God's gifts and the creativity my family has to help people. You see, when God gives you something, it's not just because He loves you; it's to pass on to others. Freely we have received; freely we will give. God has given us salvation, healing, peace, freedom, power, and love. We want to pass it on. We want to kick Satan's kingdom in the butt. We want to break strongholds with God's love. God's word never talks about retirement. We want to be going about our Father's business until He returns for us. How is this dream going to come to pass? I don't know, but God already has it figured out, and I trust Him. He will give me the desires of my heart because my heart belongs to Him.

Speaking of the desires of my heart, God granted some just recently that I have had for years. I was at a women's ministry conference when one of the speakers I had never met before started talking to me. She told me it was time to write the book God had been calling me for years to write.

She said, "The gift of writing is upon you." And if that wasn't amazing enough, she then said, "You had a miscarriage years ago, didn't you?"

"Yes," I responded in shock. Not even my mother knew about that.

"You have a beautiful girl in Heaven. She has big eyes and long, blond, curly hair. When it's your time to go home, she will be waiting with Jesus to greet you. She will be holding a big bouquet of yellow roses that she wants to give you. She spends a lot of time with a male family member in Heaven. Oh, by the way, you can name her now."

How did this woman know all of this? I always wanted to know the sex of my children so I could name them. And I knew that my children were spending time with their Pappy, and she just confirmed it. My child was excited to see me. I instantly knew her name was to be Hope. A desire of my heart was fulfilled.

Walking to my car after the conference, I said to God, "I have two children up in Heaven. What about the other one?"

"Some things are just better as a surprise," He said with a smile.

Happily Ever After

Once upon a time, there was a princess who lived in a dark and fearful land. Evil lurked around every corner. There was no beauty or color in the place she dwelled. She was cold, hungry, sick, and scared. Her clothes were tattered rags. People treated her like a pauper. She refused to look in a mirror because the ugliness in the image haunted her. She wanted to be loved but realized she was unworthy of it. Her feet had been chained since birth. She could not run or even dance. The shackles left scars on her ankles. Tears had streaked her dirty face. The sad part is the princess didn't realize that she was a princess. She believed the lies that everyone told her.

Then one day, a Prince on a white horse came riding through the streets. He was handsome, strong, and powerful. He wore a crown upon His head. People bowed as He passed by. The princess hid in a dark alley, too embarrassed to be seen. She saw people showing off for the Prince. She sat down between two garbage cans and put her head on her knees. Tears rolled down her cheeks. She was startled when she felt a hand on her arm. She looked up and realized she was looking into the eyes of the Prince. Embarrassed, she put her head back down. The Prince gently put His hand under her chin and lifted her face up. He used His sleeve to dry her tears and clean her face. He held a key and unlocked the shackles that bound her. He put His robe around her. Then He took off His crown and placed it upon her head. He embraced her. Then He escorted her out of the alley, in front of the crowd of people. He helped her up onto His horse. They rode off, out of that town.

After traveling miles and miles, they came to His kingdom. As they entered through the gates, the servants bowed down around both of them. He took her to a beautiful mansion that had mirrors everywhere. As she glanced at a mirror for the first time in years, she saw a beautiful face looking back at her. She thought her eyes were playing tricks on her. She ran to another mirror and saw the same image. The Prince stood there smiling.

"What has happened?" she asked.

"I gave you beauty from ashes. I got rid of all the ugliness, scars, sickness, and dirt from your life and showed you who you truly are," the Prince replied.

"Who am I?" she asked softly.

"You are a princess. You always have been. You are a child of the King. He created you to love, laugh, dance, run, and play. You are beautiful. You are loved. Everything He has is yours," the Prince said.

Tears poured from her eyes.

The Prince walked over and said tenderly, "I have wiped every tear from your eyes. Enter now into the joy of My Father's Kingdom."

And she lived happily ever after. How do I know this? You see, I am that princess, and Jesus is my Prince. And this story has no end.

Do you know Jesus as your Lord and Savior? This is the most important question anyone will ever ask you. Your eternity depends on your answer.

God, the Creator of everything, sent His one and only Son to the earth to take on the form of a human. Jesus lived a perfect, sinless life so that He could be the perfect sacrifice for you. He bore all your sin and shame, taking your punishment at the cross.

As it says in Isaiah 53:5, "But He was pierced for our transgressions, He was crushed for our iniquities, the punishment that brought us peace was upon Him, and by His stripes we are healed."

Why did He do this? God wanted His family back. Sin can't stand in the presence of God. The only way to redeem us and give us access to Heaven and the throne of God was for a perfect sacrifice to wash all of our sins away. So Jesus volunteered to be that sacrifice. He knew you were worth it. It is a free gift to us that cost God everything. How do you receive this gift? By faith. You could pray a prayer from your heart similar to this:

Dear God, thank you for sending Your Son, Jesus, to the earth for me. I confess that Jesus is the Son of God and that He died on the cross in my place to bear all of my sins. I believe that He rose from the grave, victorious over sin and death. I believe that Jesus is now in Heaven, sitting at the right hand of God, reigning as the King of Kings. I ask You, Jesus, to forgive me of all of my sins. I receive Your forgiveness and grace. I ask You, Jesus, to be my Lord and Savior and to come into my heart. I am Yours, and You are mine.

If you prayed this prayer…CONGRATULATIONS! All the angels in Heaven are rejoicing for you. You are now a child of the Almighty God. Your name is written in the Book of Life, and your eternity is sealed in Heaven. You get to spend forever with God and His family in His kingdom, where it is beautiful, amazing, and fun. Jesus will never leave you or forsake you. Nothing—nothing—will separate you from His love. It is important now to find a Bible-believing, Holy Spirit-filled church that is full of God's love and will help you grow. Take time to read the Bible and get to know your God. He will never quit amazing you or loving you.

The choice is yours. What are you going to do?

Tracey A. Scott is a wife and mother who firmly believes in God's remarkable power to heal old wounds. Wanting to encourage others with the hopeful message that has forever transformed her life, she felt compelled to write an account of her spiritual journey in her first book, And Then…God Showed Me His Love.

To contact Tracey, e-mail: yaygodministeries@gmail.com

Made in the USA
Middletown, DE
28 January 2017